ACTING SHAKESPEARE IS OUTRAGEOUS!

Performing the work of William Shakespeare can be daunting to new actors. Author Herb Parker posits that his work is played easier if actors think of the plays as happening out of outrageous situations, and remember just how non-realistic and presentational Shakespeare's plays were meant to be performed. The plays are driven by language and the spoken word, and the themes and plots are absolutely out of the ordinary and fantastic—the very definition of *outrageous*. With exercises, improvisations, and coaching points, *Acting Shakespeare is Outrageous!* helps actors use the words Shakespeare wrote as a tool to perform him, and to create exciting and moving performances.

Herb Parker is an Associate Professor in the Department of Communication and Performance, Theatre and Dance, with East Tennessee State University. Directing credits at ETSU include *Othello, Race, The Trojan Women, Six Characters in Search of an Author* (KCACTF "Excellence in Directing" Meritorious Achievement Award), *Caesar 2012* (his adaptation of *Julius Caesar*), *Cat on a Hot Tin Roof, As You Like It, Hamlet, A Midsummer Night's Dream* (KCACTF "Excellence in Directing" Meritorious Achievement Award) and *Little Shop of Horrors* (also a KCACTF "Excellence in Directing" Meritorious Achievement Award recipient). Professor Parker is a long-time member of the Actors Equity Association. He is the author of *A Monologue is an Outrageous Situation! How to Survive the 60-Second Audition*, published by Focal Press in 2016.

ACTING SHAKESPEARE IS OUTRAGEOUS!

PLAYING THE BARD FOR BEGINNERS

Herb Parker

Routledge
Taylor & Francis Group
NEW YORK AND LONDON

First published 2017
by Routledge
711 Third Avenue, New York, NY 10017

and by Routledge
2 Park Square, Milton Park, Abingdon, Oxon OX14 4RN

Routledge is an imprint of the Taylor & Francis Group, an informa business

© 2017 Taylor & Francis

The right of Herb Parker to be identified as the author of this work has been asserted by him in accordance with sections 77 and 78 of the Copyright, Designs and Patents Act 1988.

All rights reserved. No part of this book may be reprinted or reproduced or utilized in any form or by any electronic, mechanical, or other means, now known or hereafter invented, including photocopying and recording, or in any information storage or retrieval system, without permission in writing from the publishers.

Trademark notice: Product or corporate names may be trademarks or registered trademarks, and are used only for identification and explanation without intent to infringe.

Library of Congress Cataloging in Publication Data
Names: Parker, Herb, 1954– author.
Title: Acting Shakespeare is outrageous! : playing the bard for beginners / Herb Parker.
Description: New York : Routledge, 2017. |
Includes bibliographical references and index.
Identifiers: LCCN 2017002782| ISBN 9780415790444
(hbk : alk. paper) | ISBN 9780415790970 (pbk : alk. paper) |
ISBN 9781315212692 (ebk)
Subjects: LCSH: Shakespeare, William, 1564–1616—
Dramatic production. | Acting.
Classification: LCC PR3091 .P35 2017 | DDC 792.95—dc23
LC record available at https://lccn.loc.gov/2017002782

ISBN: 978-0-415-79044-4 (hbk)
ISBN: 978-0-415-79097-0 (pbk)
ISBN: 978-1-315-21269-2 (ebk)

Typeset in New Baskerville
by Florence Production Ltd, Stoodleigh, Devon, UK

For my brother
Harold

And in memory of
Our Sister,
Pat

How easy is a bush supposed a bear!
A Midsummer Night's Dream

CONTENTS

Acknowledgments   x

Prologue: What You Most Affect   1

   Let the Earth O'erflow   4
   So What Do I Mean, Really, by "Outrageous"?   5
   And What Do I Mean by "Caused by Love"?   7
   How Does "Outrageous" Apply to Playing Shakespeare?   8
   What You Will Find Here   10
   Before We Begin . . .   12

Act One: Shaksper Your BFF   13

   Who He was, What He Did, and What That Means for Us Actors   13
   Shakespeare's Theatre   15
       The Elizabethan Stage   16
       Shakespeare's Audience   19
   The Actor's Task   21
       All Women's Roles Played by Boys   23
       Scrolls, No Scripts!   24
   Shaksper's "Outrageous" Plays   33
       The Comedies   34
       The Histories   41
       The Tragedies   46
       The Romances   52
   Summary: What This Means for Your Acting   57

Act Two: Holding Up Mirrors — **60**

Shakespeare as a Cold Read   60
Lessons Introduction   62
Warm-up   63
Lesson 1: Doing   66
    Exercise 1: Howl   66
    Exercise 2: Sing   68
    Exercise 3: Don't Think About It   69
    Exercise 4: Hop, Kneel Crawl, and Hug!   72
    Exercise 5: Wrestle, Kick, Speak!   73
    Exercise 6: You Are Being Chased   74
    Exercise 7: Every Line is a New Discovery   75
    Exercise 8: *Become* the Words   76
Lesson 2: Verse   79
    Exercise 9: Write It in Prose   80
    Exercise 10: Tear the Words!   81
    Exercise 11: Hang Your Verse   83
    Exercise 12: Verb to Verb   85
Lesson 3: Sound   86
    Exercise 13: Gobbledygook   87
    Exercise 14: "Duh, Hell-oh, F—k!"   87
Lesson 4: Emotion   89
    Exercise 15: In-Motion, Not E-Motion   90
    Exercise 16: My Cat is Dead   94
    Exercise 17: The Last Line Six Times   98
    Exercise 18: Grow from the Ground Up   100
    Exercise 19: Roll on the Floor   101
    Exercise 20: Dueling Shakespeare   102
Summary   107

Act Three: Words, Words, Words! — **109**

    Thou *and* You   110
    The Poetry That Doesn't Rhyme   117
    The Joys of Iambic Pentameter   124
    Shared Lines   124
    A Feminine Ending   127
    More Tools from Shakespeare's Arsenal   128
    Scansion in Action   129
    Rhymed Verse and Couplets: A Poet and Do *Know It*   131

Sonnets 141
    Exercise 21: Write a Sonnet 144
Prose: How We Talk 145
Dag-nabbit! Shakespeare's Made-up Words 147
Summary 151

Act Four: Divers Schedules: A Few Items Picked Up Watching Actors Do Shakespeare   153

Item 1: There is No Subtext in Shakespeare 153
Item 2: There is Never a "Fourth Wall" 158
Item 3: Size is About More than Being Big and Loud 159
Item 4: Play What the Scene is Doing—Not Just What the Words Mean 161
Item 5: Antithesis is Fighting for an Answer by Comparing Opposites 164
    Exercise 22: Play the Antithesis 165
Item 6: Don't Report, Make a Discovery! 167
Item 7: Leave Your Hands Alone 168
Item 8: Speak a Soliloquy as if Your Life Depended upon It—Because It Does 169
Item 9: Pretty Speeches are About Blood and Guts 170
Item 10: Paint the Picture! 171
    Exercise 23: A Pig in Slop—with the Words 173
Item 11: Shakespeare is Too Big for Film 174
Item 12: All Shakespearean Characters are Philosophers and Poets 176

Postscript   178

Glossary: A Listing of Common Shakespearean Terminology   *180*
Appendix: Practice Speeches for Men and Women   *184*
Recommended Reading   *207*
Index   *209*

ACKNOWLEDGMENTS

Once again I am grateful to Focal Press and Routledge for invaluable assistance in making this book possible, especially Stacey D. Walker, Meredith Darnell, Kristina Siosyte, and Neil Dowden. In addition I want to thank Denice Hicks, Artistic Director of Nashville Shakespeare Festival, Jere Hodgin, and Dr. Robert W. Sawyer, Professor in the Department of Literature and Language, East Tennessee State University.

PROLOGUE
What You Most Affect

No profit grows where is no pleasure ta'en;
In brief, sir, study what you most affect.
(*The Taming of the Shrew*)

By all rights the acting of Shakespeare is very simple: you learn the lines and you get up on your feet and you do it. Arguably this is all he is asking of you. He has provided no long essays explaining the meaning of his great plays, he has not inserted voluminous stage directions or prologues such as you might find with George Bernard Shaw and Eugene O'Neill, and the only possible clues in acting his work that he himself has given you are those spoken by Hamlet in his advice to the players:

> Speak the speech, I pray you, as I pronounced it to you, trippingly on the tongue: but if you mouth it, as many of your players do, I had as lief the town-crier spoke my lines. Nor do not saw the air too much with your hand, thus, but use all gently; for in the very torrent, tempest, and, as I may say, the whirlwind of passion, you must acquire and beget a temperance that may give it smoothness. O, it offends me to the soul to hear a robustious periwig-pated fellow tear a passion to tatters, to very rags, to split the ears of the groundlings, who for the most part are capable of nothing but inexplicable dumb shows and noise: I would have such a fellow

whipped for o'erdoing Termagant; it out-herods Herod: pray you, avoid it. Be not too tame neither; but let your own discretion be your tutor: suit the action to the word, the word to the action; with this special observance, that you o'erstep not the modesty of nature: for anything so overdone is from the purpose of playing, whose end, both at the first and now, was and is, to hold, as 'twere, the mirror up to nature; to show virtue her own image, scorn her own image, and the very age and body of the time his form and pressure.

(*Hamlet*, Act III, Scene 2)

I cannot top that. But I am not trying to. What I hope to do is offer a few ideas for you to consider if when picking up a Shakespeare monologue or scene you are moved to ask yourself either, "What do I do now?" or "What was that again: iambic *what*?" I am guessing that this is not the first book on acting Shakespeare you will read, and I certainly hope it will not be the last; it shouldn't be. Perhaps you have already had the opportunity to act in one of his plays, though it's quite all right if you haven't. Nothing I have to say is intended to be be-all, or end-all. I am just sharing with you discoveries from some of my own struggles in working with him, both on stage as an actor and off stage as director and teacher. My hope is that if you love him as much as I do, and if you have been blessed to experience him as often as I have, some of these tips may be of use to you.

Let's say you have been handed a Shakespeare monologue or scene to perform. If you have never done this before you might be wondering how to do it; maybe your previous experience was always in a contemporary play, a play written in your own language much easier to understand. With Shakespeare you might wonder how you will be able to do it and you may be thinking that it is not possible for you to do it, that it is just too far from your ken, too removed from your own personal experience. After all, you are not British, and it's possible you have never even been to England. What might seem so daunting at first is the language—the *poetry*, page-long stanzas of verse, intermittently interrupted by blocks of what looks like prose. And those strange *words*! Weird words, from another time and place, 400 years old or thereabouts. How can you possibly make it all sound right, and make sense for you?

For help perhaps you turn to a host of Shakespeare productions on DVD. (In my day I would have resorted to listening to the old Caedmon 33 rpm vinyl recordings on a record player, but that's another story.) You find some of them quite entertaining. But still there are long stretches where it seems people are not really *talking* or *listening* to one another, at least not in the way you have been taught by Konstantin Stanislavsky[1] to do; they sometimes seem to be shouting at each other, and not just shouting but they seem to speak with such affected *accents*, as if they are more British than even the British themselves! Mistakenly this might cause you to wonder if you yourself are going to have to attempt a British accent. Is that what will make it all come together for you? Speaking this way sometimes makes them sound pompous to you, as if rather than trying to tell a great story they are trying to show you how *well* they speak, how melodic their voices sound and how long they can spew out words without having to take a breath, as if they were in a contest to see who could sound most "Shakespearean" as they declaim. You have to admit that you have also witnessed this sometimes in watching Shakespeare performed live on stage. True enough, in the scenes requiring emotion sometimes the actors do *seem* to be crying real tears, and laughing aloud with genuine joy, but how can you be sure? Is this the way it's done, you ask yourself? Is it about having a great voice? Is it about having great breath control? How do they know when to stop for a breath? How do they know what to emphasize, and what *not* to emphasize?

Finally, after much listening and viewing of Shakespeare in performance, knowing that you will have to get up and perform it soon and knowing that you must do something, you hit upon doing the one thing that you *can* do: you get by yourself—

perhaps in an empty rehearsal hall when no one is likely to discover you—you pick up the text, and you start to read ...
Aloud.

Before long, starting just this way, soon you begin to scratch at the surface of performing Shakespeare and, amazingly, in speaking it out loud following the punctuation as your guide and soon being buttressed by closer study of the text, you find out just how much is already there, in those very words, to help you with your performance. You suddenly realize that the help was right there all along, as if waiting for you, anxious to *tell* you how to play that part.

Let the Earth O'erflow

> If there were reason for these miseries,
> Then into limits could I bind my woes:
> When heaven doth weep, doth not the earth o'erflow?
> If the winds rage, doth not the sea wax mad,
> Threatening the welkin with his big-swoln face?
> And wilt thou have a reason for this coil?
> I am the sea; hark, how her sighs do blow!
> (*Titus Andronicus*)

To help my student actors make bigger, bolder choices in their acting and auditioning, I asked them in my book *A Monologue is an Outrageous Situation! How to Survive the 60-Second Audition* to think of their monologues as happening because of an outrageous situation, caused by love. I see similarities in this when performing the plays of William Shakespeare. Remember that my suggestion of "outrageous" comes from Merriam-Webster: I am asking the performer to *exceed the limits of what is usual*; to cast aside the *conventional or matter-of-fact*; to be *fantastic*. Shakespeare has no peer when it comes to this, and the themes of his plays and the situations he places his characters in more than qualifies, yes, as being caused by *love*.

I will speak about specific plays later, but I ask you: would not a mother's sons baked into a pie and served up to her for dinner qualify—putting it mildly!—as out of the *ordinary*? If this scene from *Titus Andronicus* doesn't qualify as outrageous, what does?

So What Do I Mean, Really, by "Outrageous"?

So that there is no misunderstanding, I want to make clear what I mean when I ask actors to make choices in rehearsal that are "outrageous." I am not asking them to bare their behind in the rehearsal hall, I am not asking them to perform any sexually suggestive behavior or break vow with their own faith or moral code, nor am I asking them to be rude or mean or disrespectful to their colleagues or lose control with their movements and gestures to the point that they harm themselves or other actors around them. Perhaps most importantly, I am not asking them to shout and declaim their Shakespearean performances as if they were Herbert Beerbohm Tree. These outrageous actions are intended to be *improvisational*, played by actors when rehearsing a monologue or scene in the very same way they would employ the "magic if." I therefore suggest that with your rehearsal choices you are asking:

- What would be the *unusual* thing to do?
- What would go *against* the *conventional*?
- What would be *unexpected*?
- What would go *against* the *matter-of-fact*?
- What would, to *you*, be *fantastic*?

Often in life we do the very thing that we think we would never do. We surprise even ourselves. Have you ever been in the midst of a heated argument with someone and finally been forced to shout, "I wasn't going to say anything, but—!"? After a period of stewing over some past grievance or slight you believe a friend or loved one has shown you, have you ever been suddenly triggered, by the smallest thing, to growl at them for seemingly no reason? Only to return to them later, begging, "Please forgive me. I don't know what came over me. That's not *like* me!" And in a rare moment of all-too-human frailty, maybe when you hoped no one was looking or would find out, have you ever disappointed yourself by doing something that you had always sworn you would *never* do, and perhaps in the midst of doing it could not understand what *made* you do it, even then?

This is the stuff of what it means to be flesh and blood, to be sure, but it is also what has driven the stories told in plays since Sophocles. For good or ill, human history has taught us that we frail creatures are capable of doing anything and everything, especially when we don't know why. Whatever need that is driving us is so great that we cannot keep ourselves from giving in to its power over us. So upon occasion we treat people badly, we disappoint loved ones and ourselves by doing the unthinkable. By doing what might be called *outrageous*.

When rehearsing this idea in class I provide actors with improvisations targeted at getting them to attempt the unusual and unexpected in the safety of the classroom. I also encourage them to come up with examples of their own. The actions can be stupid—perhaps *ought* to be, and they can even be out of the context of the scene, can in fact be (and this I welcome) the very thing their character would *never* do. When actors go all out and give themselves over to the "outrageous," real excitement is possible for the scene they are playing, and the hoped-for outcome is a performance richer and yes maybe even more personal than it had been before.

This is what I mean by making outrageous choices.

And What Do I Mean by "Caused by Love"?

There is no more profound emotion that drives us than the power of love. Love in the context of acting choice is inspired by every human experience you can imagine: wanted, needed, didn't have, ought to have, refused, lost and longed for, vengeful (think hate), and much more.

Just to note, however, that while most of the time this context is related to romantic love, there are other forms of love just as strong, just as likely to hurl us into outrageous action. The Greeks had six words for love:

1. *Eros.* This is sexual, passionate, romantic love.
2. *Philia.* This is love in friendship, such as loyalty among soldiers who bond as brothers/sisters in war, paying the price of sacrifice for each other, or women like Rosalind and Celia in *As You Like It.* The Greeks actually valued *philia* more than *eros*, thinking the latter ultimately ruled more by base sexual lust.
3. *Ludus.* A playful kind of love, between children and young lovers (you might imagine Romeo and Juliet, at their first meeting, beginning in *ludus* and upon the instant growing into *eros*).
4. *Agape.* Selfless love, religious, all-giving, later translated into the Latin *caritas*, or "charity."
5. *Pragma.* Long-standing love, such as between mature, long-married couples whose relationship is able to stand the test of time. This love involves compromise, patience, and tolerance of one another. Yes, *pragma* is the origin for the word "pragmatist."
6. *Philautia.* Love of *self.* While the Greeks saw value in personal respect and "love" for oneself as a means to grow and learn so as to make it possible to give greater love to others, the first iteration of this term is unhealthy narcissism and self-obsession.

I offer these historical examples to consider, but don't get bogged down by puzzling over whether your character is driven by *eros* or *agape*. A Shakespeare text will tell you that. The point is that at the heart of the outrageous situation your character finds themselves in nothing will stir the hot emotional cauldron more than what we human beings call love. In *Othello* Iago proclaims "hate" for the Moor three times in the first act. I think it can be argued that his "hate" is actually akin to love. You can decide for yourself which kind it is.

How Does "Outrageous" Apply to Acting Shakespeare?

This is the easy part, actually, because William Shakespeare has given you the outrageous in the very words he has written for you to say. He does this in his choice and contraction of words, in the made-up fantasy of words and phrases his characters speak as they struggle to live their lives. The words, dear friends! The *words!*

The following is a tragic thought, but if someone were contemplating suicide, consider the following ways such a thing might be expressed aloud:

I wonder if I should kill myself?

Then look at it the way Shakespeare chose to write it:

To be, or not to be: that is the question:
Whether 'tis nobler in the mind to suffer
The slings and arrows of outrageous fortune,
Or to take arms against a sea of troubles,
And by opposing end them? To die: to sleep;
No more; and by a sleep to say we end
The heart-ache and the thousand natural shocks
That flesh is heir to, 'tis a consummation
Devoutly to be wish'd. To die, to sleep;
To sleep: perchance to dream: ay, there's the rub;
For in that sleep of death what dreams may come
When we have shuffled off this mortal coil,
Must give us pause: there's the respect
That makes calamity of so long life;
For who would bear the whips and scorns of time,
The oppressor's wrong, the proud man's contumely,

> The pangs of despised love, the law's delay,
> The insolence of office and the spurns
> That patient merit of the unworthy takes,
> When he himself might his quietus make
> With a bare bodkin? who would fardels bear,
> To grunt and sweat under a weary life,
> But that the dread of something after death,
> The undiscover'd country from whose bourn
> No traveller returns, puzzles the will
> And makes us rather bear those ills we have
> Than fly to others that we know not of?
> Thus conscience does make cowards of us all;
> And thus the native hue of resolution
> Is sicklied o'er with the pale cast of thought,
> And enterprises of great pith and moment
> With this regard their currents turn awry,
> And lose the name of action.

Now of course any statement weighing such a question is a terrible tragedy, no matter what words are used. Both statements listed above are unspeakable on their face, and there are countless ways such an awful deliberation can be played by an actor. But in rehearsal, after sifting through all the ways to play the scene, you are trying to find the *best* choice, the singular choice that will resonate with the greatest amount of effect upon you as well as the audience. The first one listed above is short, simple, and unthinkable. The second, written by Shakespeare, is just as troubling, but with a very important exception: in Hamlet's brooding speech Shakespeare does what he always does; he helps the actor to live in the *moment* of the play even as he is posing a terrible, philosophical question *to the audience.* With his words Shakespeare breathes life into his characters and at the same time he challenges the audience to consider questions of the human condition so universal they are almost impossible to be answered and yet, because of our humanity, they must be asked, and out loud. They are questions that will be asked for all time and are certainly being asked even now, long after they were first put on paper.

This is why William Shakespeare is the greatest playwright who ever lived.

His text, his images, and the case he makes to his audience more than demonstrates the actions of people driven to outrageous behavior because of outrageous situations. And, on the lighter side, don't forget that this applies to his comedies, as well, as his characters express joy and happiness so limitless that it too is inexpressible, yet somehow—because they are so happy!—they have simply got to at least try to express it.

Boy, do they ever try!

What You Will Find Here

This is what you will find in the book to help you: Act One "Shaksper Your BFF" is a refresher about who the man was (from what little we know about him) and how the way theatre was done in the 1600s may have influenced his writing—and therefore how this can offer you tips on how to act him; Act Two "Holding Up Mirrors" offers exercises and improvisations to get you on your feet playing with him; Act Three "Words, Words, Words!" delves into the sometimes giddy arithmetic of his poetic structure, principally iambic pentameter, and Act Four "Divers Schedules" lists a few things about acting Shakespeare I have personally learned over the years. I assure you, you will find no mystery in any of this. You will quickly discover that I have tried to keep historical theories (such as who wrote the plays, for instance) to a minimum; such questions will not be answered here nor should they be the most important concerns for you. First, last and always, think about how you are going to *get up on your feet and act him right now, and how doing this can help make your performance believable.* I have included some Shakespeare monologues in the back of the book for practice and a glossary of many of the strange and confusing terms you will keep running into as you read his plays. Please refer to them but don't let them get in the way of the speech or scene you are working on right now; nothing must slow down that process. Before this book is finished you will find me saying constantly that with Shakespeare the most important thing is to memorize his lines as quickly as possible and then get up to rehearse, *even if at first you do not understand what you are saying*. Naturally you will never do this in actual performance; this notion is about working on him through improvisational trial and error rehearsal. Of course you must know what you are saying and why; this is the only way to reach an honest and nuanced performance, speaking those words, yes, as if you were a human being *just talking*, as if they were your very own words and they had just come to you for the first time at that moment. You must be able to speak them with the *ease* of a contemporary play even though you are not doing a contemporary play; you must seem, frankly, to be *real*, even though you are telling a story so unreal it has risen to heights never before imagined in theatrical history. How do you start? You can begin with the text, where you will find all you need to know about your role, all the truth, motivation, and emotion required to "hold the mirror up to nature." Shakespeare has done so much of the work for you already that it is not unfair to suggest, in the end, that all you really need to do is "say the words."

One more note I might make for clarification, friends. Often here you will see me talk about the drama in terms of thea*ter* and thea*tre*. What I mean is this: think of thea*ter* as the *building* where we work; and consider thea*tre* as the *art* we hope to honor and create.

Before We Begin . . .

One of the best acting notes I ever received after a performance was not from a director or another actor or even from someone in theatre. It was from a town local, a country boy as I will characterize him. He spoke with a home-spun drawl and it was clear that he knew nothing at all about Shakespeare, but he had come to see the play—which was *A Midsummer Night's Dream*, in which I played Puck—and he enjoyed it. He knew someone in the cast so I had occasion to sit near him at a bar after the show, and in the pinpoint, perceptive way that only people without a preconceived agenda but rather an innate sense to somehow understand what they are seeing can do, he said to me: "You were good in that play. Seem like them lines *come real easy to you.*"

Best acting note I ever got.

I hope that some of the ideas you find here will make Shakespeare's lines come at least a little easier to you. I hope they will come out of you as simply and honestly as you can make them, and I am convinced that at least one way to get there is through fearlessly playing with his words and images and situations *on your feet.*

This said I would still like to whisper into your ear one last thought that I believe will be instructive to you on this journey, which is meant to serve your acting needs in general as well as "doing Shakespeare" in particular. If you would be so kind, knowing full well that I am not the inventor of this thought, and at the risk of being obvious and realizing that the actor's research will always need to be done, please always think about the following when you pick up any of Shakespeare's plays: they were written to be *performed*, not *read*.

Herb Parker

---

1 Konstantin Stanislavsky (1863–1938) was a famed Russian director and acting teacher who founded the Moscow Art Theatre and established actor training philosophy that included physical actions, emotional memory, and the "magic if." In the United States his teaching came to be called "The Method."

Act One

SHAKSPER YOUR BFF[1]

> Be not afraid of greatness. Some are born great, some achieve greatness, and some have greatness thrust upon 'em.
>
> (*Twelfth Night*)

Who He Was, What He Did, and What That Means for Us Actors

Given how much he has been lauded, studied, criticized, and analyzed over the centuries it might be argued that knowing as little as we do about the man named William Shakespeare is, well, outrageous. It may even be just as fantastic when you learn that one of the things that we have been able to document about him is that his surname, during and after his lifetime, was spelled some 80 different ways, ranging from "Shappere" to "Shaxberd."

What we seem to be reasonably sure of is that he was born to John Shakespeare and Mary Arden and was baptized at Holy Trinity Church on April 26, 1564 in Stratford-on-Avon, England. April 23 is the day accepted as his birthday and this is the day we celebrate. We do know that in 1583 at the age of 18 he quickly married 26-year-old Anne Hathaway and his first child, Susanna, was born six months later. The twins Hamnet and Judith (1585), named after two of Shakespeare's friends, followed. Sadly, Hamnet died in 1596. One of the things that we don't know is what happened to young Will from the years 1583 to 1592, often referred to as the "Lost Years," though he did seem to have gotten busy writing in 1593 with the publication of the epic poems *Venus and Adonis* and *The Rape of Lucrece*. He spent most of his working life in London while his family remained in Stratford, which has led to speculation that his marriage was not happy, but he did support them long distance and visited them from time to time, at least once a year. Otherwise there are no surviving letters or records, by either of them or by people who would have known them, to fully indicate what the couple's relationship was like. By 1598 he was at work in earnest with the Lord Chamberlain's Men (later renamed the King's Men in favor of King James I after Queen Elizabeth's death). We cannot be absolutely certain what his first play was, but scholars, using historical events alluded to in the plays, records of performances, possible publication dates, and when the plays finally appeared first in print, suggest that it may have been *Henry VI, Part 2*, probably written between 1589 and 1590 and perhaps first performed at the Rose Theatre in London. By the time the company built the famous Globe Theatre in 1599 the young man who was eventually dubbed the "Bard of Avon" was well on his way. The Globe burned to the ground in 1613 but was rebuilt in 1614. Shakespeare appears to have retired a wealthy landowner to his home called New Place in Stratford, and lived there until his death in 1616.

Today we pretty much accept that William Shakespeare wrote the plays for which he is given credit. Over the centuries of course there have been rampant theories that in fact he did not write them, the argument being that one man of such relatively humble grammar school education who never attended university could not possibly have had such grasp of the human condition, let alone language (even though part of his primary schooling would have included Latin grammar). A wide variety of people have been proposed as the true writer of the plays, including Sir Francis Bacon, Sir Walter Raleigh, rival Christopher

Marlowe (who died in a tavern brawl in 1593), Edward de Vere the Earl of Oxford, Roger Manners the 5th Earl of Rutland, the Countess of Pembroke Mary Sidney Herbert, and even—believe it or not—Queen Elizabeth I, and this is not the full list.

For myself I don't really care if he wrote them or not. I am simply grateful that these toweringly transcendent plays, which had to be culled together seven years after Shakespeare's death by his friends John Hemminge and Henry Condell for inclusion into the First Folio, survive and exist for us to enjoy today. That is all that I care about.

I assure you that this section is not intended to make a Shakespeare scholar of you; college libraries and now the internet are chock full of massive tomes on the life and work of William Shakespeare for you to peruse if you so desire. In fact my own hunch is that even the Bard himself, who seems to have never overseen publication of his own plays in his lifetime, wouldn't spend his time doing that himself. What we are about here is getting you on your feet as quickly as possible to start acting him. But toward that end, a bit of context and information can be instructive. It might help you even more to accept the possibility that acting Shakespeare is out of the ordinary, is fantastic, and is, well, *outrageous* . . .

Shakespeare's Theatre

To act Shakespeare it is useful if you study how theatre was done in Shakespeare's day. You do this for clues on how the times might have influenced the way he wrote and how that would have affected the way his actors interpreted what he wrote. You do not do this so that you can do Shakespeare "exactly as he would have done it"; that would be impossible. For one thing the theatre venues of today dwarf those available to Shakespeare in size, scope, variety, and technology. Theatrical performance in his time was vastly different, one of the big differences being— and you know this already—that the great women's roles,

Beatrice, Rosalind, Juliet, Lady Macbeth, et al.—were played by young men and pre-pubescent boys. So, going in you realize that full replication is not what you are after. But you can trust that in this history you will unearth tidbits that will *inform* what he wrote, and this insight will inform your performance as well, so that you can at least approach the *spirit* of what he was trying to do.

So you knuckle down, and you start digging.

The Elizabethan Stage

How about the stage on which you would actually be performing? Well, a theater such as the Globe would be in a hexagonally shaped, three-story building with a great hole in the roof (the "Wooden O" spoken of by the Chorus in *Henry V*). Inside there would be seating for as many as two thousand and perhaps even three thousand people. Along the sides would be tiered galleries and balconies where the rich and the powerful would sit, paying nearly two pennies for this privilege. There would also be seating on the floor before the stage, but space immediately in front of the stage, up close, called the *pit*, was where the poor would stand and view the play for the price of a single penny (approximately 10 percent of a day laborer's pay). They would stand on the ground close to the stage edge, so they would come to be called, of course, "groundlings," as well as "penny stinkers," because of poor personal hygiene associated with their low social status. The stage itself, some 5 feet high, would jut forward in nearly a three-quarter thrust and the actors would make entrances through curtained doors to the left, center, and right (known as the "discovery place"). These doors led to the tiring house backstage where the actors could change costume. We can only estimate but the Globe stage dimensions might have ranged from 20 feet wide by 15 feet deep to 45 feet to 30 feet, either way a vast space for actors to traverse. There would be a trap door in the floor center stage and above the stage rose a balcony supported on pillars which would also have a trap. In Figure 1

ACT ONE: SHAKSPER YOUR BFF

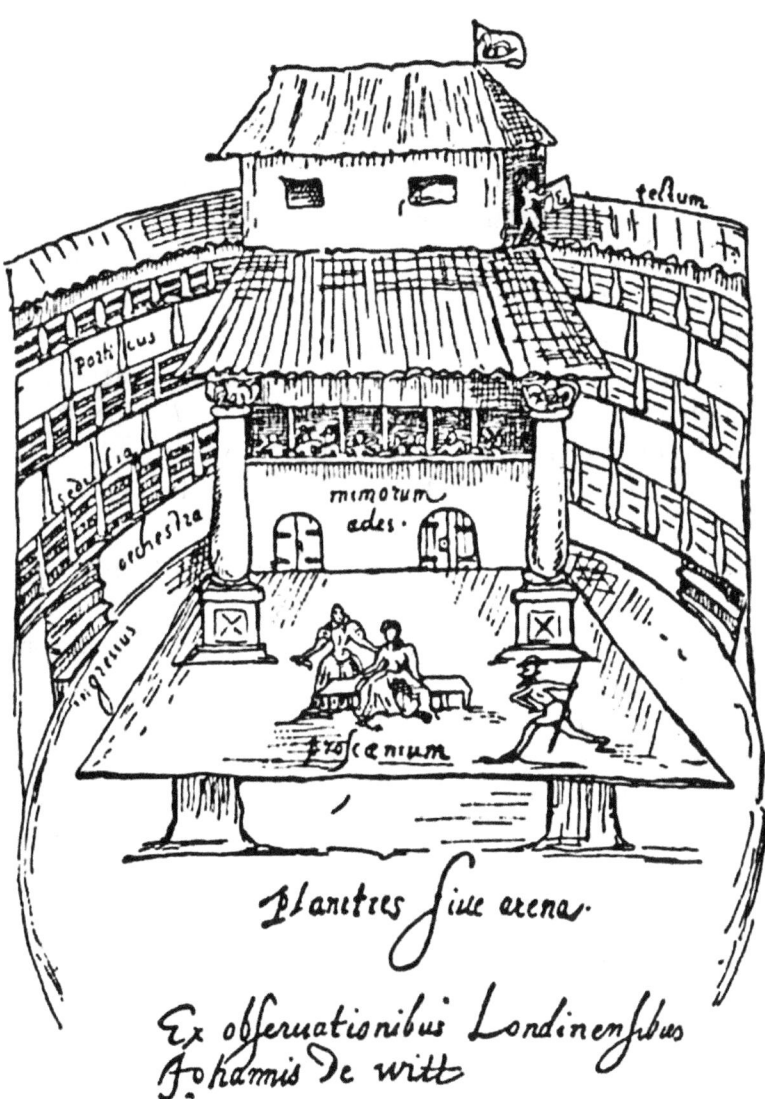

Figure 1 The Swan Theatre, circa 1596. Arnoldus Buchelius (1565–1641), after a drawing of Johannes de Witt (1566–1622).

you can see a 1596 drawing of a performance in progress at the Swan Theatre, which will give you an idea of how the Globe was configured.

This type of stage would be your "setting," no matter what kind of play you were performing. Today we can boast lavish theatrical scenery that can be flown in from intricate fly systems, changing the scene as many times as a play requires, but not in Shakespeare's time. His bare stage would have to represent everywhere his players had to travel, from the Forest of Arden to a league outside of Athens to the countryside in Scotland or England or Agincourt, and more. It would also signify the senate of *Julius Caesar* and the ominous Bohemian desert where Antigonus met his fate at the hands of a bear in *The Winter's Tale*.

There were no playbills or programs as we know them now, but leaflets might be handed out to announce the performance that day. The company might also hoist a flag high atop the theater to make the announcement as well, with the flag's color indicating what type of play it was going to be: black for tragedy, white for comedy, and red for history. A trumpet would sound to alert everyone that the performance was about to begin. Inside the theater placards would be placed at the side of the stage to introduce a scene. If the scene called for furniture, chairs, benches, or beds might be carried on here and there but this would be the only visible stage furniture the audience would be able to see with their eyes during the performance, and sometimes in hasty exits even these pieces might be just left behind on the stage as the next scene was going on. To help the spectators further "see it," Shakespeare naturally would describe his settings in detail in the text: how it should look and smell and even how the wind would blow for Lear or the sea storm rage to shipwreck Viola in *Twelfth Night* or Prospero's foes in *The Tempest*.

The plays would have been performed on this bare stage in the afternoon during the summer months, possibly two o'clock, making indoor lighting, which they did not have anyway, unnecessary. This was also referred to as "universal lighting," which allowed the actors to see the audience as well as the audience to see the actors, the genesis of the presentational, Elizabethan style of acting so suited to Shakespeare's plays. Indoor lighting by candle was reserved for the eventual indoor buildings during the winter. The audience would be situated above you, in front of you, and on both sides of you. The actors had to speak up to them and down to them and on both sides to them, and of course there was no front curtain. This made it necessary for all of the scenes in Shakespeare's plays to end with the actors simply walking off or being carried off if the characters had been mortally injured or otherwise slain. Also, because of the large deep stage Shakespeare's actors played on, great energy was required to move about quickly from one side of the stage to the other so that you could present the play to as many people as possible. Actors might even have occasion to enter from the aisles, having to elbow their way past the unruly clientele to get back up onto the stage; there was no need to pretend that the audience "wasn't there." You would never be hiding from the audience the fact that everyone in the galleries and on the ground was there to see a play, witnessing performers as they quickly "strutted their hour" upon those boards.

Shakespeare's Audience

Shakespeare's audience included the poor and the illiterate as well as the rich and the powerful. The poor viewed the plays from the ground. Much farther back, higher up in galleries, sat the very rich, privileged, and powerful. The exception to this was Queen Elizabeth, who could not be seen to be mingling among commoners; the Lord Chamberlain's Men came to perform for her at Greenwich and Whitehall, and later the King's Men played in front of King James I at Hampton Court. Imagine if your performances could expect the president of the United States to be in attendance. Huddled in that same public audience would be a cross-section of the entire population, more than half of whom would have not been able to read or write.

For entertainment fare, Elizabethans would have been accustomed to attending such spectacles as public beheadings, cockfighting and bear-baiting (this last was a particular favorite of Queen Elizabeth). They would have been used to making constant noise and commotion during the course of the show, pushing and shoving during the play, and would have freely tossed objects at the actors on stage (the term "egg on your face" comes to mind, as it has been suggested that unruly playgoers might have thrown them, among other things, at actors to express their displeasure with a performance). Sometimes a special admission price would have allowed wealthy patrons to sit on the very edge of the stage itself, and because they were often there to be seen as well as see the play distraction for the audience and actors alike was caused. This would demand that actors speak ever more clearly, directly to them, for the audience had no written reference to refer to. Thus it becomes that the playing of Shakespeare is earthy and gritty, not just aesthetic; you are not in a parlor/salon of the French Restoration pronouncing witty poetic rhymes for amusement as you play badminton among a few private friends. For Shakespeare's audience, considering that the most horrific events of the day could be looked on as routine pastime, this increased the appetite for more "realistic" depictions of carnage in the more violent plays of his canon (such as *Titus Andronicus*, which was popular for this very reason), leading to the use of such things as pig's blood and entrails, sheep's lungs, heart, and liver, all to help make the grisly moments more "believable." (Of course this desire for such shocking realism has remained very much a part of live theatre throughout the centuries, a twentieth-century example being the David Rabe play *Streamers*, in which an actor wore a blood-pack vest underneath his shirt so that the audience could see blood spurt from his wounds as a soldier stabbed him on stage.) This made it necessary to perform Shakespeare's plays with (almost literally) the very blood and guts of life, even while speaking words fraught with the beauty and universality no writer had ever infused into them before.

Going to the theater was as much of a sporting event to the Elizabethans as UFC fighting, WWE Wresting, and the National Football League is to us in the New Millennium. Afford Shakespeare's text the weight it rightly deserves, to be sure, but remember that you are also telling a story to mass onlookers as varied in social strata as our own vast teeming cities. Suppose, for instance, that of a night in the Metropolitan Opera House at the Lincoln Center in New York City you could spy both the homeless as well as the rich, right alongside each other? Both of them viewing well-known stories handed down from legend and popular culture for generations, as homespun and down to earth as *Snow White and the Seven Dwarfs* or *The Three Little Pigs*.

The Actor's Task

If that may be, then all is well. Come, sit down, every mother's son, and rehearse your parts. Pyramus, you begin: when you have spoken your speech, enter into that brake: and so everyone according to his cue.

(Peter Quince, *A Midsummer Night's Dream*)

As an actor with a theatrical troupe of the day you would have probably gotten up at dawn, had a paltry breakfast consisting of perhaps porridge and cheese (think of coffee and a bagel in our time), and then you would rush to the Globe. If in fact you were a member of one of the theatre troupes licensed by sponsorship at the time (such as the Lord Chamberlain's Men, for example, patronized by the Lord Chamberlain of Queen Elizabeth), you would have been very lucky. Otherwise you would have had to scrounge from hand to mouth by performing in countryside taverns, inns, or on the back of wagon-wheel stages of the time, while generally keeping yourself scarce lest you were caught without papers by the officials, who looked down upon actors as vagrants and ne'er-do-wells. But as a "part player" with a company, you could have expected to bring in a daily wage of about a shilling a day. This was not as much as the main player

Figure 2 Will Kempe (*right*), from the cover of *Nine Daie's Wonder,* circa 1600.

wage of two shillings a day, but it was pay. Eventually, if you became famous and in demand—such as Richard Burbage, Will Kempe, Edward Alleyn, et al.—you might have become a stakeholder (business partner) in the Globe and this would have made you wealthy indeed.

At the Globe there would not have been a stage manager in the sense that we have come to know them. Instead there would have been a theater manager, often called a prompter, who would have had all of the "cue" scripts in his possession after they had been approved by the Master of Revels (a court official with the power to choose and censor plays for performance). This prompter would have been charged with handing you your "part." Before the performance you would also read over the *platt* (perhaps a version of the word *plot*), a piece of paper nailed to the wall backstage listing the order of scenes, entrances and exits, dances and fights during the performance (our call board).

Listed here you would also find out whether or not you would be called upon to rise up from the trap in the stage floor below to signify Beelzebub, or Hecate, or the gravedigger, or if you would have to lower yourself from the trap in the balcony above the stage in order to play God or an angel, or Ariel, or Puck. The entire society of people who made theatre happen in Shakespeare's time understood this and embraced it as the way plays were performed. Think of it: as an actor in the company all you had to be concerned with was getting your lines down and saying them out loud when your cue came. Imagine that!

All Women's Roles Played by Boys

In Shakespeare's time the women's parts were of course played by young boys and men. You know this already. There are varying reasons for this, much of the thought generally being that the theatre profession was just too lascivious and immoral a vocation for women of good character to participate in—even though women did apparently appear in masques and pageants of the time. Women did not finally act on the English stage until after Charles II reopened London theaters with the Restoration of 1660. The first documented performance was by Margaret Hughes (1630–1719), playing the role of Desdemona in *Othello*. But before that, the roles went to boys who were apprenticed to the acting troupe and provided with room, board, and an allowance. These "boy players" would be taken under the wing of elder actors in the company to be trained and most of them grew to male roles as their voices changed. Though the Elizabethan audience was fond of plot twists that entailed disguise, the actor-changing-costume-quickly side of me can't help but theorize that these twists might have been employed by Shakespeare out of a desire to give a bit of *relief* to his female-playing actors by establishing the amazing conceit of young men playing women who disguise themselves as men. We see this in his plays *As You Like It, The Merchant of Venice, The Two Gentlemen of Verona, Twelfth Night*, and *Cymbeline*. But no matter how well some of these young men were able to pretend to be women—and there were a few who became quite famous and adept at it, one being Alexander Cooke (died 1613), famously thought to have created many of Shakespeare's heroines—what you as an actor can take from this fact is that the performance style of the day, beyond culture and social mores of the time, first last and always, was meant to be *non-realistic*. This is no small consideration in the acting of Shakespeare's plays, even though women's roles are now played by women and even though Shakespeare himself would not have categorized his work as realistic or non-realistic (realism as a genre did not become part of dramatic literature until the nineteenth century). Shakespeare simply wrote for the people of his time in the form that dramatists employed at the time. There were unfortunate hazards to boys playing the women's roles, however. The white make-up used to portray women was lead-based and poisonous, causing many of the young men to contract skin disease and some to even die of lead poisoning. But just as much as the audience did, even actors themselves had to make the leap of faith to accept the stage convention of males as females, and this recognition further brings home the nature of the material you are working on. This conceit includes the fact that you are telling a story by speaking *poetry*: a reality "heightened" by necessity to help your acting reach the kind of heights required to be seen and understood in the vast open theater houses for which Shakespeare wrote.

Scrolls, No Scripts!

A theatre company such as the King's Men or Lord Chamberlain's Men might produce as many as 11 plays in two weeks' time. This was in an attempt to make more money by turning over plays as rapidly as possible and beating other companies to the punch for the paying audience. As such, there was very little time for rehearsal. In some extreme cases actors might not have gotten their part until the play was already in progress, and some did not even get scripts at all—their few lines were whispered to them by a prompter backstage just before they were to say them. This came to be called "cue acting," which eventually gave way to cue "scripting," in which the actor is only given their own lines.

Today we call them sides, the term we use for musical scores and scripts rented out by such publishers as Music Theatre International, the Rodgers & Hammerstein Organization, and Tams-Witmark, but in Shakespeare's day they would have been called *scrolls*—small, rolled-up sheets of parchment paper attached to a stick of wood on which his actors would have been distributed their parts. (This practice we trace to the origin of actors referring to their parts as "roles.") Today publishers of musical scores and librettos divvy them out in these small portions to protect intellectual property and copyright. In Shakespeare's time such laws did not exist; upon completion of his play Shakespeare (as all Elizabethan playwrights) would have sold his script to the owner of the theatre troupe. Bits and pieces of popular scripts were routinely stolen, recopied and recycled, then remounted under another author's name. (Some brazen souls even wrote Shakespeare's name on their stolen play-scraps to pass themselves off as him; this in turn may account for the many different spellings of his last name.) Therefore the company manager could better keep tabs on owning his property—*Hamlet*, let us say—if the number of "cue" script copies was kept to the absolute minimum. For that matter it was very expensive to reproduce copies of plays in Shakespeare's time. William Caxton introduced the printing press to England in 1476, but the process was still painstaking and slow even a hundred years later because the type was set using small letters in block form that could get mislaid or even run out of supply. This might also be one of the reasons it was so time-consuming and maddening when Shakespeare's colleagues got together to put all of his plays into publication in the First Folio, and what accounts for the thousands of errors, misspellings, and punctuation confusion among all of the editions over the centuries. (Although I suppose this might argue even more evidence of the greatness of

Shakespeare's plays. Their universality and beauty was still able to survive, even with the mistakes of well-intentioned editors who survived him!)

But when you think about it, why would it be necessary to have a full copy of the text anyway? You were not going to read over the entire play later to study it for historical or literary value. You would not be going over it to try to divine the theme or the spine of the piece, nor would you be trying to discover the super-objective of your character or your objective in each individual scene. Any obstacles that might be in your character's way would be self-evident in the words you were reading, and those same words would even be telling you how to speak the lines.

As an actor what you would be doing, then, at this first hasty reading, would be trying as quickly as possible to just memorize your part. This makes it clearer than ever that Shakespeare's plays were written to be performed, not studied or analyzed. Study and analysis came long after he was gone!

So each actor was handed a scroll that contained *only* their role, consisting of the last two or three words spoken by the previous character before their first line of dialogue. This is how your entire part would have been laid out, and large or small, short or long, this scroll would tell you what and how to say the words you had been given; they would tell you where you were, who you were, what circumstances you had been placed in, and exactly what you were feeling at the moment. Handy, don't you think? This would enable the play to unfold right before your eyes, just as it would before the audience.

Below is my admittedly humble attempt to replicate a possible cue script. *You* are playing Oberon:

Enter, from one side, OBERON, with his train; from the other, TITANIA, with hers.

OBERON
    Ill met by moonlight, proud Titania.

ACT ONE: SHAKSPER YOUR BFF

TITANIA
_____ bed and company.

OBERON
Tarry, rash wanton: am not I thy lord?

TITANIA
_____ joy and prosperity.

OBERON
How canst thou thus for shame, Titania,
Glance at my credit with Hippolyta,
Knowing I know thy love to Theseus?
Didst thou not lead him through the glimmering night
From Perigenia, whom he ravished?
And make him with fair AEgle break his faith,
With Ariadne and Antiopa?

TITANIA
_____ parents and
    original.

OBERON
Do you amend it then; it lies in you:
Why should Titania cross her Oberon?
I do but beg a little changeling boy,
To be my henchman.

TITANIA
_____ part with him.

OBERON
How long within this wood intend you stay?

TITANIA
_____ spare your haunts.

OBERON
Give me that boy, and I will go with thee.

TITANIA
_____ I longer stay.

Exit TITANIA with her train.

Next is an example of the same scene, playing Titania:

Enter, from one side, OBERON, with his train; from the other, TITANIA, with hers.

OBERON

　　_____ moonlight, proud Titania.

TITANIA

　　What, jealous Oberon! Fairies, skip hence:
　　I have forsworn his bed and company.

OBERON

　　_____ I thy lord?

TITANIA

　　Then I must be thy lady: but I know
　　When thou hast stolen away from fairy land,
　　And in the shape of Corin sat all day,
　　Playing on pipes of corn and versing love
　　To amorous Phillida. Why art thou here,
　　Come from the farthest Steppe of India?
　　But that, forsooth, the bouncing Amazon,
　　Your buskin'd mistress and your warrior love,
　　To Theseus must be wedded, and you come
　　To give their bed joy and prosperity.

OBERON

　　_____ Ariadne and Antiopa?

TITANIA

　　These are the forgeries of jealousy:
　　And never, since the middle summer's spring,
　　Met we on hill, in dale, forest or mead,
　　By paved fountain or by rushy brook,
　　Or in the beached margent of the sea,
　　To dance our ringlets to the whistling wind,
　　But with thy brawls thou hast disturb'd our sport.

Therefore the winds, piping to us in vain,
As in revenge, have suck'd up from the sea
Contagious fogs; which falling in the land
Have every pelting river made so proud
That they have overborne their continents:
The ox hath therefore stretch'd his yoke in vain,
The ploughman lost his sweat, and the green corn
Hath rotted ere his youth attain'd a beard;
The fold stands empty in the drowned field,
And crows are fatted with the murrion flock;
The nine men's morris is fill'd up with mud,
And the quaint mazes in the wanton green
For lack of tread are undistinguishable:
The human mortals want their winter here;
No night is now with hymn or carol blest:
Therefore the moon, the governess of floods,
Pale in her anger, washes all the air,
That rheumatic diseases do abound:
And thorough this distemperature we see
The seasons alter: hoary-headed frosts
Far in the fresh lap of the crimson rose,
And on old Hiems' thin and icy crown
An odorous chaplet of sweet summer buds
Is, as in mockery, set: the spring, the summer,
The childing autumn, angry winter, change
Their wonted liveries, and the mazed world,
By their increase, now knows not which is which:
And this same progeny of evils comes
From our debate, from our dissension;
We are their parents and original.

OBERON
                              _____ be my henchman.

TITANIA
    Set your heart at rest:
    The fairy land buys not the child of me.

His mother was a votaress of my order:
And, in the spiced Indian air, by night,
Full often hath she gossip'd by my side,
And sat with me on Neptune's yellow sands,
Marking the embarked traders on the flood,
When we have laugh'd to see the sails conceive
And grow big-bellied with the wanton wind;
Which she, with pretty and with swimming gait
Following,—her womb then rich with my young squire,—
Would imitate, and sail upon the land,
To fetch me trifles, and return again,
As from a voyage, rich with merchandise.
But she, being mortal, of that boy did die;
And for her sake do I rear up her boy,
And for her sake I will not part with him.

OBERON

_____ intend you stay?

TITANIA

Perchance till after Theseus' wedding-day.
If you will patiently dance in our round
And see our moonlight revels, go with us;
If not, shun me, and I will spare your haunts.

OBERON

_____ go with thee.

TITANIA

Not for thy fairy kingdom. Fairies, away!
We shall chide downright, if I longer stay.

Exit TITANIA with her train.

When playing a role, just think of how truly alive and energized your performance could become; suppose you truly had *no idea* of what the other character was going to say until they said it? Suppose you had to *hang upon their every word*, listening intently, either from the wings or waiting on stage as they spoke, waiting for those last three words to cue you? Being forced to play the scene this way will certainly compel you to *listen* with hyper-sensitivity; you will have to because you do not know how long the speech will last before you speak. Sometimes inexperienced actors "drop out" if they do not have many (or any) lines in a scene in which they must remain on stage while other characters are speaking; and admittedly it can be a challenge—as well as energy-draining—to keep listening, to stay *in the scene*. Working with a script such as this can certainly help with this challenge. Does not this almost compare to being in the midst of a Meisner exercise, genuinely listening and acting only when the moment demands it, using material produced long before Sanford Meisner[2] was even born? No longer will you be listening for just a "cue" alone, you will be genuinely hearing a conversation *for the first time*. This is also why actors were tasked to memorize their words as quickly as possible, for a performance might have happened that very afternoon. Further—and this is the point—scripts laid out this way makes analysis of the words, incomplete anyway because you don't have a complete script, *folly*. Shakespeare has already infused the meaning into the poetic meter (we'll talk more about this later). All you had to do was say it.

Now to acting on a thrust stage. Because of being surrounded by spectators on three sides, you will not be playing to the kind of "fourth wall" box-set configuration as you would play to in a proscenium theater. This reality is a good acting note even if you are performing on a stage that *has* a "fourth" wall; the sensorial understanding that someone is always watching you, particularly from behind, fosters in the mind of the actor the vital theatrical convention of *sharing* the play with the audience. In the theatre for which Shakespeare wrote you are *telling* a story as well as *living* a story, and this will further demand that you *play the house*, which will mean delivering the story to each and every person. Think of the Boy or Girl Scouts sitting around a campfire telling ghost stories. They desire to build suspense in the hearts of their young listeners as they look into the fire-lit eyes of amazed Scouts around them, checking to see if they are being drawn into the tale, trying to paint a picture for everyone listening so that when the fateful moment in the story comes they might jump out of their seats. On a much grander scale, Shakespeare's plays are trying to do the same thing. Even as Titus Andronicus is sinking into madness bred out of despair, he is recounting his every feeling and thought directly to the audience. Shakespeare's plays are stories being told very much like radio dramas were before the advent of television. His audience knew they were going to *hear* a play every bit as much as *see* a play. Your vocal instrument would have had to be sturdy in an attempt to make sure the audience—especially since they could get so unruly—could hear and understand you, but also because your desire to *tell that story* would have raised the required energy level even more.

Again: everything the audience had to know to enjoy the play—to *hear* the play—would have been placed in the mouths of actors speaking directly to them. This cannot be said often enough to the modern-day actor struggling to make sense of Shakespearean text. The way you make sense of it is to get up on your feet and speak it aloud (oops, I said it again), as if performing for more than a thousand people during an afternoon at two o'clock. The two o'clock hour is also instructive; it would have been at this time of day that you were supposed to believe that soldiers on the watch during the dead of night were frightened by a ghost in the opening scene of *Hamlet*. How would the audience be able to accept that it was so dark? Because Shakespeare engaged their imagination with the words. His words would have never been more vital during an afternoon hour when every play was at the mercy of the elements, whether blinding sun or torrential rain streaming through the open roof. What Samuel Taylor Coleridge would later call "the willing suspension of disbelief" just might have begun with Shakespeare's words.

Shaksper's "Outrageous" Plays

The great dramatic works that have stood the test of time involve plots that on their face can be thought outrageous in at least some way. There I go, harping on this outrageous thing again. But think about it: Sophocles of course started it all, setting the bar very high with *Oedipus Rex*, in which the hero learns that he has killed his father and married his mother. Outrageous, don't you think? This continues in our great dramatic literature today; from two hobos seemingly waiting for a friend who never appears in *Waiting for Godot*, to a down-trodden salesman named Willy Loman in *Death of a Salesman* who faces tragedy because he had the "phony dream" that all it took to make it big in American society was to be "well liked." Arguably it can even be found when Felix Unger moves in with Oscar Madison in Neil Simon's *The Odd Couple* and Nellie Forbush struggles to overcome racism for love of Emile De Becque in *South Pacific*.

Taking stories from legend and mythology that came before him, William Shakespeare fashioned a body of work that speaks to this outrageous situation caused by love for all time, and of course he infused this into his delightful comedies as well. Here, in what is generally accepted to be the order of their completion and the categories in which they have been ascribed, are Shakespeare's plays and a listing of just how unconventional his stories can get. For an example, how's this: Shakespeare wrote 13 comedies[3], and only *one* of them takes place in England!

I do not provide these synopses to let you off the hook from reading the plays—rather, I hope that discovering something of what happens in them will make you want to read them even more, and, better yet, pick up each text and start speaking the words aloud. The following plot listings can never replace what you will learn once you start reading the greatest playwright the world has ever known. This includes when he wasn't writing at his best, or, even, when he had *help* . . .

One other quick mention: six of these works I refer to as "problem plays." Don't let it worry you. Over the centuries a few scholarly folks have had questions when in their view some of the plots did not get wrapped up as tidily as others. English critic Frederick Samuel Boas chose three of them in 1896: *All's Well That Ends Well*, *Measure for Measure*, and *Troilus and Cressida*. Three others, *The Winter's Tale*, *Timon of Athens*, and *The Merchant of Venice*, were added to the list years later. Suffice it to say that for an actor's purposes, a "problem play" is simply going to be when a comedy doesn't seem to end all that happily and a question of marriage or social justice is not as clear by play's end as you might think it would be. I assure you it won't interfere with your acting choices one bit. My guess is that these questions might even add a little extra juice to your search for the fantastic, the unexpected, and the out of the ordinary—that is to say, for the *outrageous*.

The Comedies

1589

THE COMEDY OF ERRORS

Two sets of twins, one set rich and privileged (Antipholus of Ephesus and Antipholus of Syracuse) and the other set poor and brought up to serve them (Dromio of Ephesus and Dromio of Syracuse), are paired together and separated at birth. After much confusion and mistaken identity in which Ephesus's wife mistakes Syracuse as her husband and Syracuse woos Ephesus's wife's sister (are you not getting confused already?), the adult Dromios are at last introduced to one another and the Antipholi are reunited with their father and mother (who had become a nun), just in time to save the life of the father, sentenced to death because he is a Syracusan merchant who broke the law by entering the city of Ephesus. You are of course treated to a happy ending.

1593

THE TAMING OF THE SHREW

Baptista Minola of Padua must marry off his eldest daughter before his youngest can be wed. Bianca, the youngest, is wooed by three suitors: Hortensio, Gremio, and Lucentio (who disguises himself as a tutor so that he can be close enough to Bianca to pursue her in private). Lucentio's manservant Tranio disguises himself as his master to thwart the other two suitors. Petruchio of Verona, with an eye on the very large dowry, woos the elder Katherina (called Kate the "Curst") by killing her with "kindness" (which consists of sleep deprivation, starvation, and what amounts to what today we might consider mental cruelty), eventually winning her over. By play's end, though, the story suggests to us that it might actually be the (seemingly) demure baby sister Bianca who will ultimately give her husband the most trouble by being a "hellcat," not Katherina. Having been "tamed" and speaking of course for women of the sixteenth century, in the final scene Kate delivers a long diatribe in which she orders women to be submissive to their husbands. Admittedly, this speech can sometimes be problematic for contemporary actresses even to this day. Perhaps that is why this moment is so often played to the audience with a wink and a *nod*.

THE TWO GENTLEMEN OF VERONA

Valentine confesses to his friend Proteus that he and Silvia plan to elope, but Proteus has secretly fallen in love with Silvia. Julia, Proteus's former love, leaves Verona for Milan in disguise as a boy named Sebastian, trying to find Proteus. Proteus sends his pageboy Sebastian (Julia) with a ring to Silvia in exchange for a picture of herself in further proof of his love. Silvia seeks out Proteus in Milan and is captured by outlaws; Proteus rescues her; he and Valentine quarrel and are reconciled. Julia, who has followed, misunderstands their reconciliation and faints;

Proteus sees the ring he gave her and as soon as her true identity is revealed his love for her is returned. Valentine is reunited with Julia and Proteus with Silvia and to conclude this confusing fantastic plot there is a Shakespearean double wedding.

LOVE'S LABOUR'S LOST

King Ferdinand and his three best buddies swear a vow to devote themselves to three years of strict scholarship and study, during which time they will not have anything to do with women. As it happens the Princess of France appears with her three best maidens, to discuss matters of state with the king. Berowne, one of the king's friends, falls in love with Rosaline, one of the Princess's ladies, and secretly sends her a letter. At the same time his three brethren including the king have all been smitten by the Princess's other maidens and realize how futile it was to eschew the company of women. At a masked ball they disguise themselves as Russians as a joke but wind up wooing the wrong women. All is revealed happily until news is received of the death of the Princess's father, the King of France. The Princess and her ladies must refuse marriage to their beloved men until a year of mourning for the departed king has passed.

1595

A MIDSUMMER NIGHT'S DREAM

Two sets of lovers flee to the woods outside of Athens, one to escape the law and the other to pursue them. At the same time in that very forest a group of "rude mechanicals" are rehearsing a play to honor Duke Theseus on his wedding to Queen Hippolyta. Along the way both lovers and mechanicals are set upon by the mischievous fairy Puck (a.k.a. Robin Goodfellow), servant to Oberon, king of the fairies. Puck charms the young lovers into falling in love with each other, transforms Nick Bottom, the leader of the mechanicals, into an ass (donkey, and play on the word "Bottom," get it?) just in time for the Fairy Queen Titania to fall in love with him at first sight (as Oberon, out of vengeance because she has denied him a changeling child, has devised). However, all is made magically well by the by play's end, and one of the funniest comic interludes in the history of theatre—the play-within-the-play *Pyramus and Thisbe*—delights both actors and audience alike. A famous theme is found in the line "The course of true love never did run smooth."

1596

THE MERCHANT OF VENICE

A persecuted Jewish money lender seeks revenge upon a businessman who owes him money by proposing to cut out his heart, earning a "pound of flesh" for the debt. The day is saved, however, when the rich maiden Portia (who is betrothed to the debtor's best friend) and her lady in waiting, both fantastically dressed as men, show up in court to plead the case for the debtor. Shylock is defeated and forced to become a Christian. Last of the original problem plays, the question of whether or not this play is fundamentally anti-Semitic rages to this day, though this notion is contradicted by the fact that the "Hath not a Jew eyes?" speech is one of the most moving pleas for religious tolerance in Shakespeare.

1598

MUCH ADO ABOUT NOTHING

Two witty acquaintances, Benedick and Beatrice, renowned for trading sarcastic and biting barbs at one another, are tricked by friends into believing that they are actually in love with each other. They then save the marriage of Claudio and Hero by convincing the young groom his bride-to-be is dead (out of grief over being falsely accused of adultery, which Claudio was tricked into believing by the conniving Don John, bastard brother of Don Pedro, Prince of Aragon). Claudio is told that his false accusation can be sponged if he marries her "twin"—the very same young virgin Hero whom he had cast aside earlier in the play. All ends happily, of course, and there is another Shakespearean double wedding. The "ass" Constable of the Watch Dogberry (perhaps originally played by Will Kempe) is another comedic gem introduced by William Shakespeare.

1599

TWELFTH NIGHT

Viola, a high-born young lady—who happens to have a twin brother—is shipwrecked in Illyria, believing her brother lost at sea. She dresses up as a boy and begins work for Duke Orsino, whom she falls in love with. Thinking Viola is a good young male servant he sends her to woo local beauty Olivia on his behalf. Olivia has been in mourning for her father's death but the young "man" (the shipwrecked beauty Viola in disguise) wins her heart. As it happens, Viola's twin brother Sebastian appears in Illyria, and, since he is (as an actual man) the spitting image of his disguised sister, much confusion ensues over the young woman and her brother, but all problems are solved with the young woman matched to her duke and her twin brother with the mourning maiden. The puritan, stuck-up Malvolio, servant to Olivia, is yet another great Shakespearean comic creation.

AS YOU LIKE IT

To escape death at the hands of her evil uncle, a young maiden named Rosalind dresses as a boy and flees to the woods of Arden with her lifelong friend and companion Celia, herself in disguise. It so happens Rosalind runs into the strapping young man Orlando whom she fell in love with back at court, who himself is fleeing death at the hands of his evil brother Oliver. Along the way the young disguised woman is pursued by Phebe, a local lovesick country girl, but everybody ends up with their rightful mate once her true identity is revealed and her best friend is smitten and betrothed to Orlando's previously evil brother Oliver, who has turned over a new leaf. You can imagine that a double wedding is in the offing. The melancholy Jaques speaks the "seven ages of man" speech, rightfully one of the most lauded in all of Shakespeare. And Rosalind poses this famous question: "Why then, can one desire too much of a good thing?"

THE MERRY WIVES OF WINDSOR

It is believed that Queen Elizabeth convinced Shakespeare to write this play in order to bring back Falstaff after killing him off in *Henry V*. This totally fluffy romp involves the massively fat Sir John wooing two women of the town behind their husbands' backs. The two merry wives Mistress Ford and Mistress Page actually are wise to the rotund knight's tricks and exert their joyous vengeance upon him for the entire play, in one instance whisking him out of the house away from the wildly jealous Master Ford in a laundry basket that gets dumped into the Thames. By the end all is forgiven, of course, and everyone enjoys a cup of sack together.

1601

TROILUS AND CRESSIDA

Achilles is preventing the Greek army from battle with the Trojans because he refuses to fight and will only listen to his friend, Patroclus. The Priestess Cassandra prophesies destruction from war with the Greeks but is ignored. Troilus is no longer interested in war, having met and sworn his love to Cressida, as her father joins the Greek side. Pandarus had arranged for the two of them to meet and they spend the night together, vowing eternal faithfulness. Hector is set to take on any Greek in man-to-man combat and "brainless" Ajax is chosen but the eventual battle is inconclusive. Against her will, Cressida is sent by her father back to the Greek camp, where she is wooed by Diomedes. Thinking that she will never see Troilus again, she returns Diomedes' affections by bestowing Troilus's own love tokens upon Diomedes. Certain that he has lost Cressida's love, Troilus returns to fight against the Greeks, his brother Hector is slain in battle by Achilles' soldiers, and Troilus laments the loss of the woman to whom he had sworn everlasting love, Cressida. On Boas's list *Troilus* is the first of the problem plays.

1602

ALL'S WELL THAT ENDS WELL

Helena is a young maiden of the lower class who happens to possess power to heal the sick. She also has fallen in love with the soldier Bertram, who will have nothing to do with her. Helena heals the ailing King of France and, because the king has promised her whatever she wishes for doing so, grants her the hand of Bertram in marriage. Bertram is forced to obey his king and marries her, but out of spite he then goes off to war before their marriage can be consummated. After much machination Helena is brought to Bertram's bed in disguise as the prostitute he *thinks* he is sleeping with. Their union is consummated and when the ruse is revealed at play's end, inexplicably, Bertram pledges love for Helena, whom he has shunned for the previous five acts. Number one on Boas's list. Talk about a "problem" play!

1604

MEASURE FOR MEASURE

Isabella is bent upon being a nun. Angelo has been handed the rule of the realm by Duke Vincentio while he leaves the country on business. Strict laws prevent sex before marriage; as it happens, Isabella's brother is guilty of violating this law and is sentenced to death. However, Angelo, in power, has the authority to pardon him, so Isabella goes to Angelo to plead for her brother's life. What she does not know is that Angelo is a secret, lust-filled cad himself, and he will only grant Isabella's brother clemency if she agrees to have sex with him. She refuses, and tries to reconcile her brother to impending death. Duke Angelo, all this time, has been secretly suspicious that Angelo is not as pious as he has claimed, and the duke has dressed himself up as a monk to keep an eye on the blackguard Angelo. Claudio does not die, of course; he is given pardon and will be married to the young lady he had relations with. With a twist at the end of the play that makes one's head spin, the duke reveals himself and then turns around and *proposes marriage* to Isabella—remember she was so devoted to God that she was willing to condemn her own brother to death. Will she agree to marry the duke? Shakespeare has given her no answer in words at the end of the play. Some might consider this a "problem."

The Histories

1590

HENRY VI, PART 2

The kingdom of England is in chaos, with warring factions vying for power and position. The king's arranged marriage to Margaret provides no dowry, the Earls of Warwick and Salisbury are convinced that Richard Plantagenet (father to the eventual King Richard III) has a rightful claim to the English throne, and the worthy Duke of Gloucester's wife Eleanor is arrested as a traitor and then banished after being duped into trying to get a witch to summon demons. Richard raises an army against King Henry; Richard's forces win victory and King Henry flees. Then the plot *really* thickens.

HENRY VI, PART 3

Richard Plantagenet is sitting on King Henry's throne, supported by the Earl of Warwick. The king begs for the throne back, vowing to bequeath the kingship to Richard after his death. Margaret, Queen to King Henry, raises an army when she hears of this. York's sons Edward and the future Richard the Third insist their father assume the throne and fight. They lose and Edward's head is set on a pike at the gates of York. The sons continue to fight and eventually prevail, and Edward of York is crowned King Edward IV; the deposed King Henry is sent to the Tower of London. More plotting, scheming, and arranged marriage ensues, leading to King Henry being returned to the throne, then deposed again by Edward and tossed back into the Tower, where he is eventually murdered by Richard of Gloucester. This confusing trilogy concludes, setting in motion the plot of the play *Richard the III*.

1591

HENRY VI, PART 1

This play begins the War of the Roses trilogy with the choosing of red or white roses by the warring houses of Lancaster or York to identify each side. We are introduced to Richard, Duke of York (the future Richard III), and a highly Anglicized (one-sided) portrayal of Joan of Arc (called "La Pucelle" in the play) and the kingdom of England changes hands through war and strife without a resolution to this first part. If you try to figure out why *Henry VI, Part 1* appeared *after* the first two parts it will make you dizzy; just accept that the first two came, were successful, and then finally *Part 1* was offered up as a prequel. Is your head spinning at this?

1592

RICHARD III

The hunchbacked, deformed Duke of Gloucester plots to kill all of his enemies—including his relatives—in order to become king of England. He woos and wins the hand of Lady Anne, even though it was he who killed her father (King Henry VI) and her husband (Edward the elder Prince of Wales), delivering one of the most fantastical proclamations of love in all of Shakespeare, at the very foot of Edward's coffin. Others who meet death at the hands of Richard are his own brother George, Duke of Clarence, the young Edward, Prince of Wales, and Richard, Duke of York (boys whom he had killed in the Tower of London), Lords Rivers, Grey, Hastings, and Buckingham (who serves him loyally until Richard turns on him). You might already know his most famous speech: "A horse! A horse! My kingdom for a horse!"

1595

RICHARD II

King Richard II banishes both Henry Bolingbroke (the future King Henry IV) and Duke of Norfolk to settle a dispute between them. John of Gaunt (Richard's uncle and Bolingbroke's father) dies and King Richard takes his lands. An army is raised against him and the returned Bolingbroke takes him back from Wales to London, where Bolingbroke usurps the crown and sends Richard to the Tower of London. Bolingbroke becomes king amid great strife and turmoil, leading him to cry out loud for escape from the imprisoned Richard. Thinking they are acting on the king's orders, soldiers go to the Tower and kill the deposed King Richard, cursing the reign of Henry IV and setting in motion the series of plays that follow.

1596

KING JOHN

John shakily assumes the throne after the death of his brother Richard the Lionheart. King Phillip of France insists the crown be given to John's nephew, Arthur. King John tries to smooth things over by an arranged marriage but is excommunicated by the Pope. After a battle Arthur is captured by the king's army. King John tries to have Arthur murdered. The young boy Arthur convinces his would-be murderer to spare his life but the child falls to his death trying to escape. Bloody war between the Dauphin and English forces ensues with no resolution. King John, perhaps poisoned, dies.

1597

HENRY IV, PART 1

Henry IV's troubled reign as King of England continues but the real plot of this play is: 1) the reconciliation (in my mind not unlike Biff Loman to Willy Loman in *Death of a Salesman*) between King Henry and his wayward prodigal son Prince Hal; and 2) the introduction of one of Shakespeare's most beloved characters, Sir John Falstaff. War is declared on the king by forces led by Henry Percy and his son, called Hotspur. Shakespeare continues his expert fast-and-loose play with history and contrives to set up a kind of "high noon"-type battle between the two disparate sons, Hal and Hotspur, with Hal winning permanent glory by killing the assumed better fighter Hotspur on the field of battle at Shrewsbury. (In history, however, it is not actually known how Hotspur died, and in any event Hotspur was actually 23 years older in age than Prince Hal and two years older than King Henry IV himself.) But the audience's love of country embodied by heroic Prince Hal and love of the scheming, lying, fat, and cowardly Sir John Falstaff is also established forever.

HENRY IV, PART 2

It is three years after the events of *Henry IV, Part 1*. Prince Hal seems to have reverted back to his old carousing with Sir John Falstaff, at the Boar's Head Inn. The ailing King Henry calls all officers to war. Unfortunately this includes the ever-conniving, larcenous Falstaff, who instead of recruiting soldiers as he has been charged, cheats Justice Shallow out of his money and allows his would-be soldiers to buy their way out of service. At this same time, Prince Hal has already begun to distance himself from Sir John. After a final reconciliation with his son, King Henry IV dies. At play's end the young Prince Hal becomes Henry V, and displaying royal maturity he has not shown before, he renounces his old bad influence Sir John Falstaff, who feebly tries to laugh off the repudiation.

1598

HENRY V

This is a romanticized recounting of the brief reign of England's King Henry V. Points of history, chronology, and facts are fictionalized for dramatic effect. What is also notable is, through a tremendously moving prose speech by a grieving Mistress Quickly, the recounting of the last days and death of Sir John Falstaff. The young actor Laurence Olivier, who makes a brilliant film of this play in 1944, uses the St. Crispin's Day speech to rouse British troops against Hitler during World War II. Perhaps, understandably, this is why his film of the play has been called the "best propaganda film ever made."

1613

HENRY VIII

It is generally accepted that Shakespeare collaborated on this play with John Fletcher. You know the history: Henry VIII falls in love with Ann Bullen [sic], a lady-in-waiting at court. Though he has been married to Queen Katherine for 20 years he decides that the marriage is incest because she is the widow of his dead brother. The king goes to Cardinal Wolsey for advice but Wolsey is widely hated in the kingdom and cannot support the king's plea for a divorce, and instead sends the question to the Pope. However, because he is so despised and plotted against, Wolsey loses what favor he had possessed with the king, who now sees Wolsey as standing in the way of the divorce. Wolsey has asked the Pope to postpone a decision, but the king goes ahead with the divorce and remarriage. After delivering the most memorable speech in the play—and certainly among the best speeches of Shakespeare's canon, the "So farewell to the little good you bear me" speech in Act III, Scene 2—Wolsey dies, followed soon after by Katherine. You know what happens. Anne Bullen, before she herself is accused of treason and then executed, delivers a daughter who will one day become Queen Elizabeth. Cranmer is given a speech by Shakespeare which seems to glorify the reign of Elizabeth: "She shall be, to the happiness of England / An aged princess . . ."

The Tragedies

1593

TITUS ANDRONICUS

A great Roman general's family tragedy is set in motion after he returns triumphant to Rome having defeated the Goths and captured their Queen Tamora along with her sons and followers. For trying to prevent an arranged marriage between Titus's only daughter Lavinia and ruler Saturninus, Titus's eldest son is banished and his youngest son is killed by Titus's own hand. The virginal Lavinia is kidnapped and raped by Tamora's sons, who cut out her tongue so that she cannot say who did it, and cut off her hands so that she cannot write their names. The evil sons arrange to trap two more of Titus's sons and frame them for the murder of Lavinia's husband-to-be. Titus is duped by Aaron the Moor into chopping off his own hand, thinking it will win clemency for his condemned sons, but this fails and they are executed anyway by ruler Saturninus. Titus gets even, though, by slitting the throats of Tamora's two boys, baking their bodies into a pie and forcing her to eat it. As I have said, this was one of Shakespeare's most popular plays during his lifetime.

1594

ROMEO AND JULIET

Two teenagers, who happen to be from families that are sworn enemies, meet at a party and fall into everlasting love. They are married in secret. After a brawl during which relatives of the Prince of Verona as well as the Capulets have been killed (not to mention his own friend Mercutio), the young husband is banished from the city. The young wife, in a jam because her father has ordered her into an arranged marriage, rushes for help to the friar who had married them in secret; thinking that it will help he gives her a potion which will cause her to seem dead, thus getting her out of the marriage. The friar tries unsuccessfully to get word to the young man that his wife is not dead and will wake from the potion. The young husband, thinking she is really dead, kills himself in her tomb. She wakes just as the potion wears off, only to find him dead; she kills herself with his dagger. Though this is too late, all of this brings their warring parents together in peace. The play is of course chock-full of famous speeches, including "What light through yonder window breaks," "Gallop apace, you fiery-footed steeds," and "Romeo, Romeo, wherefore art thou Romeo?"

JULIUS CAESAR

Loosely retold from Plutarch, the fall of Julius Caesar is chronicled through his death at the hands of conspirators led by the noble Brutus, who is later undone by Marc Antony. Caesar's fall is foretold by a Soothsayer begging him to "beware the ides of March." In addition, Brutus's fall is foreshadowed by the appearance of the ghost of the murdered Caesar. Suicide and death ensues for both Brutus and the "lean and hungry"-looking Cassius, and all of the conspirators. Famous speeches include "Friends, Romans, countrymen, lend me your ears!" And who does not know what the mortally stabbed Caesar is asking of his old friend when he whispers, "Et tu, Brute?"

1600

HAMLET

"Something is rotten in the state of Denmark" when the good King Hamlet is murdered by his evil brother Claudius. The ghost of the king appears to his namesake son, and the young prince's course of confusion and fear, resolve and revenge begins. He puts on a play to prove the guilt of his uncle, accidentally kills Polonius (the father of his lady love Ophelia) thinking that he has caught Claudius listening in on his private accusation with his mother Gertrude. Hamlet is finally goaded into a duel with Laertes, son of the dead Polonius and brother to Ophelia (who drowned herself in madness out of grief over the death of her father). Claudius and Laertes plot Hamlet's death at the sword contest by both dipping the tip of Laertes' foil in deadly poison and poisoning a cup of wine meant for Hamlet at the contest. Sadly, his mother Gertrude drinks from it, dies, and Hamlet and Laertes are both mortally wounded by the poisoned blade. But at least Hamlet gets his vengeance upon Claudius by forcing him to drink the poisoned wine that is left before he stabs him. Suggested to be about both existentialism and the Oedipus complex, few doubt that *Hamlet* is the greatest of Shakespeare's plays, and very likely the greatest ever written.

1604

OTHELLO

Because Desdemona's handmaiden Emilia does not reveal that she found her lady's lost handkerchief and gave it to her husband Iago, Desdemona is murdered in her bed by her husband, the great general Othello, a blackamoor leading the army in Venice. Othello has been duped—amazingly—by his second in command Iago into believing that she has committed adultery with his lieutenant, Michael Cassio. One of Shakespeare's greatest tragedies, perhaps the greatest question in dramatic literature is: why was Othello the Moor of Venice so *gullible?*

1605

TIMON OF ATHENS

A man who is foolish enough to lavish all of his wealth upon his friends, thinking that they will come to his rescue when he is in need, is cruelly disappointed, so he then decides to renounce all of mankind, donning filthy sackcloth and hiding himself in a distant cave. To this difficult play's further ruin, no real female love interests exist in the story save for two prostitutes, which I have a "problem" with. But even so, there are still a few fine Shakespearean speeches to listen to.

KING LEAR

The King of England turns his crown and power over to his three daughters, out of a desire "to shake all cares and business from our age; / Conferring them on younger strengths, while we / Unburthen'd crawl toward death." His youngest daughter, whom he loved the most, is the most honest and cannot force herself to compliment him just for political gain; he disowns her and turns the kingdom over to his two elder daughters, who, of course, hate him and immediately plot his downfall. Setting in motion one of the most extensive subplots in Shakespeare, along the way one of his trusted advisors Gloucester is duped by his bastard son Edmund into thinking his favorite legitimate son Edgar has betrayed him, and he is then blinded by evil daughter Goneril's husband and henchmen and cast into the wilderness (one of the most harrowing scenes you will see on stage). Edgar, on the run for fear of death at his father's hand, pretends to be mad and becomes "Poor Tom," also in the wilderness. In this same wood the newly mad Lear, driven insane by his children, runs into them both. His favorite daughter Cordelia returns with an army and they rescue Lear, only to be captured by Goneril and Regan's army. The Fool mysteriously disappears in Act III. In prison Lear's beloved daughter is murdered and he enters carrying her, uttering his "Howl, howl, howl, howl!" speech (don't forget to check out the exercise in Act Two of the book). When he laments "My fool is hanged," he is actually referring to Cordelia. (This is one of the reasons the two roles are sometimes doubled.) Lear dies after. During the play some famous lines Shakespeare introduces to us include "Nothing will come of nothing" and "How sharper than a serpent's tooth it is to have a thankless child!"

1606

MACBETH

Three witches (also "weird" or "wayward" sisters) appear to Macbeth after he has won a great battle and tell him that he will become King of Scotland. But they also tell his partner Banquo that he will be the father of a great line of kings, which leads to Macbeth and Lady Macbeth's long course of murder which begins with the both of them stabbing King Duncan upstairs in their house. The blood spilled on their hands is never able to be washed off. Soon King Macbeth can no longer sleep, and he is visited by the ghost of Banquo, whom he had killed. Lady

Macbeth goes mad and dies and Macbeth is killed by Macduff because Macduff, as prophesied by the weird sisters, was born by cesarean section. Among the famous lines: "Unsex me here," "Screw your courage to the sticking place and we'll not fail," and "Thou are the best o' the cutthroats!"

ANTONY AND CLEOPATRA

In middle age, Mark Antony and Queen Cleopatra are in the midst of a tempestuous affair. News of the death of Antony's wife Fulvia causes him to return to Rome, as Pompey is plotting war. To cement the Roman alliance, Antony agrees to marry Octavius Caesar's sister, Octavia. All know this will not end Antony's affair with Cleopatra. War with Pompey is avoided but then the truce is broken and Octavius Caesar defeats Pompey. Soon it is feared that Octavius will go to war against Antony because of his continuing affair with Cleopatra. Both men raise armies and commence war. Against better judgment Antony allows Cleopatra to command a warship at sea and Antony's forces lose the battle when Cleopatra's ship flees, leaving them vulnerable. Antony is distraught with Cleopatra, but this changes after she sends false word that she has killed herself. Antony, out of grief, falls on his own sword, killing himself. Cleopatra is captured by invading Octavius, but before he can parade her through Rome as a prisoner she is helped by her handmaidens to kill herself with the bite of an asp. In his one conciliation Octavius Caesar has Antony buried next to his Cleopatra. Enobarbus, Antony's lieutenant, has a famous speech before his own suicide.

1608

CORIOLANUS

The great Roman warrior Caius Martius Coriolanus defeats the Volscians and is given a hero's welcome when he returns to Rome. His name is put forward for the position of consul, but he must plead to the plebeians for their votes, something the proud Coriolanus finds distasteful but agrees to do. The common people first grant him their votes but then change their minds, which enrages Coriolanus, who condemns the government of Rome. He is declared a traitor and forced into exile. To exact revenge Coriolanus offers his services to the Volscian army, to its leader Tulus Aufidius, whom he had defeated earlier. The Volscian army is on the brink of war with Rome. Only his mother Volumnia's pleading convinces Coriolanus to relent from attacking Rome. He does finally relent and returns to Antium, but Aufidius accuses Coriolanus of treason, and Coriolanus is assassinated.

The Romances

1607

PERICLES

Pericles, Prince of Tyre, discovers that King Antiochus and his daughter, whose hand in marriage Pericles had competed for, are engaged in incest. King Antiochus marks Pericles for death, causing him to flee. Pericles' ship to Pentopolis capsizes, with Pericles being the only survivor. While there he meets and falls in love with Thaisa, daughter of Simonides, marrying her. With Antiochus' death Pericles is able to return to Tyre with his now pregnant wife Thaisa. During passage Thaisa gives birth to a girl, whom Pericles names Marina. But Thaisa seems to die in the process and Pericles, grieving, seals Thaisa's body in a watertight coffin and buries her at sea. The coffin eventually floats to Ephesus, where Thaisa is revived by Cerimon. Fearing that her husband has been lost at sea, Thaisa commits herself to a life as a nun. In the meantime Pericles has given Marina over to be raised by the governor of Tarsus and his wife, Dionyza. As happens in *The Winter's Tale*, 16 years pass. Marina grows to a beautiful woman but is the object of Dionyza's jealousy.

Dionyza plots to kill the young woman. She is taken away by ship, but before she can be killed she is kidnapped by pirates. Cleon builds a monument to her. Pericles visits Tarsus and upon seeing the monument he is overtaken with grief. The pirates have sold Marina to a brothel in Mytilene, but she is set free by Lysimachus, that state's governor. Pericles makes his way to Mytilene and finds his daughter, speaking to her without realizing who she is. When he finally does recognize her he rejoices at their reunion, Lysimachus proposes marriage to Marina and Pericles is told in a dream that he must journey to Ephesus. He takes Marina with him and there they meet Thaisa, now a head priestess, and the family is happily back together again.

1609

THE WINTER'S TALE

Consumed by jealousy, Leontes, King of Sicilia, is convinced that his pregnant wife Hermione has been unfaithful to him with his old friend Polixenes, King of Bohemia. Bent on revenge, he orders his loyal servant Camillo to poison Polixenes. Camillo instead warns Polixenes and they flee Sicilia. Leontes is convinced that his wife's unborn child is illegitimate and throws her into prison. In the meantime his young son, by her, dies. When Hermione's baby, a girl, is born Leontes orders the infant be taken to the wilderness and left there to die. The Oracle at Delphi proclaims that both Polixenes and Hermione are innocent of infidelity. Hermione collapses over the death of her son and is spirited away by her loyal handmaiden Paulina, and is soon believed dead herself. Hermione's baby was left on the coast of Bohemia by Antigonus, Paulina's husband, who is eaten by a bear. A Shepherd finds the infant and raises her, giving the child the name Perdita. Sixteen years pass. Perdita has grown to a beautiful young woman and Prince Florizel, son of Polixenes, sees her and falls in love. Leontes has changed after all this time and has been grieving over his believed deceased wife. Paulina has just completed a statue of Hermione to honor her memory and she invites the entire court, Leontes and Polixenes and young betrothed lovers, to attend the unveiling. At the unveiling the statue of Hermione comes to life, and Leontes and she are reunited at play's end. The middle of Act III, Scene 2 contains the famous editor-added stage direction, *"Exit, pursued by a bear."* Always categorized as a romance, years after it first appeared scholars chose to dub it a "problem play" as well.

1610

CYMBELINE

Good King Cymbeline has married a disagreeable woman as his queen. Cymbeline has arranged for his daughter Imogen to marry the queen's son Cloten, but Imogen defies her father and marries the low-born but worthy Posthumus. An angry Cymbeline banishes Posthumus, but not before giving his young wife Imogen a bracelet; she in turn gives him a diamond ring which he vows to wear faithfully. The evil Iachimo convinces Posthumus to wager the ring against his wife's fidelity, but when Iachimo goes to Britain in the hope of seducing Imogen he is unsuccessful. While Imogen is asleep Iachimo steals the precious bracelet from her and shows it to Posthumus, convincing him that his wife has been unfaithful. Enraged, Posthumus orders his manservant Pisanio to kill Imogen. Instead, because he believes Imogen to be innocent, Pisanio disguises her as a page and helps her flee from the court. What ensues is the introduction of two grown sons of Cymbeline, living in secret for 20 years. The evil Cloten appears at the dwelling of the two sons disguised as Posthumus and in a battle with one of the sons is beheaded. Imogen takes a potion meant to be poisonous (from the scheming queen) but it only stupefies her thanks to the virtuous physician Cornelius rendering it harmless. The brothers think Imogen dead and take her to the woods, placing her body next to Cloten's headless body, spreading flowers about them. Imogen awakes thinking (because of the familiar clothing) that her husband Posthumus is dead. After many comedic romantic twists and turns, Iachimo confesses his foul deeds, mistaken identities are revealed and the lovers reunited.

1611

THE TEMPEST

A deposed Duke of Milan, Prospero, after many years in exile on a desolate island, has the chance to exact revenge against his brother Antonio, King Alonso and members of their party by using his magical mystical powers to cause a shipwreck. His enemies are cast onto the island, in the hands of Prospero. Also cast upon the isle is the strapping handsome young Ferdinand, son of King Alonso who fears his son has perished at sea. Prospero's daughter Miranda has never seen a man save for her father on the island and immediately falls in love with Ferdinand. He in turn falls for her. While this is going on, the bitter part-man-part-fish Caliban tries to get back at his master Prospero by aligning with the clowns Trinculo and Stephano. (Caliban has been his slave since Prospero vanquished the evil witch Sycorax, an action that also set free his other "good" slave, Ariel.) Their comedic machinations fail, Prospero forgives the old enemies who deposed him, and Ferdinand and Miranda are betrothed. The play is notable for its belief that it was Shakespeare's last solo play, with passages especially at the end that suggest a master playwright "drowning his book." Famous lines include "We are such stuff as dreams are made on, and our little life is rounded with a sleep."

1613

THE TWO NOBLE KINSMEN

Not always considered as part of the canon, this play is also believed to have been written with the collaboration of John

Fletcher. Probably taken from Chaucer's *Knight's Tale*, the two title characters are Palamon and Arcite, who have been captured fighting for Thebes against Athens. In prison the two men are attracted to Emilia, the sister of Hippolyta, wife of Theseus. They both vow to woo her even though they have previously vowed eternal friendship. Eventually Arcite is exiled from Athens and Palamon is left in jail. Once free, Arcite disguises himself as a peasant to keep an eye on Emilia. At the same time the jailer's daughter has fallen in love with Palamon. She helps him to escape, hiding him in a forest nearby. Arcite discovers him there and again they fight over Emilia, deciding to duel that night. But before they can duel Theseus encounters them. He condemns them to death but both Emilia and Hippolyta convince him to banish them instead. The two noble kinsmen refuse, however, so Theseus demands that Emilia choose between them, with whoever loses the duel being put to death. When Emilia cannot decide which one she chooses Theseus declares the matter will be decided by combat in one month, both men vying for Emilia's hand, the loser to be executed. Because of her unrequited love for Palamon the jailer's daughter has gone mad. Theseus pardons the deranged daughter and her father for allowing him to escape. Thinking his scheme will restore her sanity, a doctor gets the man to whom she's engaged to pretend to be Palamon. Arcite defeats Palamon in the contest, but before he can be executed a messenger arrives bringing news that Arcite has been mortally wounded in a horse-riding accident. Before he dies, Arcite gives Emilia's hand to Palamon.

* * *

The sources of Shakespeare's plays are extensive, and include *Plutarch's Lives* (from which he derived material for his "Roman" plays *Julius Caesar, Antony and Cleopatra, Coriolanus,* and *Timon of Athens*) and Ovid's *Metamorphoses*, which helped him put together

Titus Andronicus and *A Midsummer Night's Dream.* For historical plays he referred to Raphael Holinshed's *Chronicles of England, Scotland and Ireland,* among others. He also took material from Giovanni Boccaccio's *The Decameron* for such plays as *All's Well That Ends Well, Cymbeline,* and *The Two Gentlemen of Verona. The Tragical History of Romeus and Juliet,* a poem by Arthur Brooke, appears to have inspired *Romeo and Juliet.*

With the exception of *King Edward III* (1595), *Sir Thomas More* (1603), *Cardenio* (1613–14, with John Fletcher), and the recently discovered *Double Falsehood* (deemed in 2010 to be reliably taken from lost Shakespeare manuscripts and adapted by Lewis Theobald in 1727), these plays represent what we can fairly acknowledge to be Shakespeare's canon. It is notable that, of the accepted 37, only *Love's Labour's Lost* and *The Tempest* contain plots created totally by Shakespeare himself.

But the fact that he didn't make up his own stories is, putting it mildly, beside the point. We will of course never know how the original source material would have stood the test of time, but we can certainly judge the resulting plays that came from his pen.

Which would *you* rather read?

Summary: What This Means for Your Acting

Okay. You have a bit of background on Shakespeare's life and how theatre was done in his lifetime. For the actor trying to bring these great roles to life in an art form devoted first to entertainment and only later to critical conjecture, in the beginning stages of your rehearsal I urge you to simply say the words aloud, and you will be more than halfway there in being faithful to what we can surmise he originally intended. And, at least in the beginning, I really do mean *say* them; please don't fall into the trap of *Shakespearean* acting. Your ultimate goal is to present to the audience a *believable* human being in *un*believable situations who just *happens* to speak poetry as their native tongue. An actor cannot play a theory, nor is it reliable to attempt subtext, whether it is there or not; an actor can only *do* something to *get* something, and through the unfolding of the story it is left to the audience to figure out what possible theme might be subliminally there. All the actor ever need do is *play the play*.

After you have found the outrageous possibilities in your work (I hope by considering the exercises in Act Two), it will admittedly be necessary to study to help you play the role. Shakespeare will present you with age-old language and culture his actors did not have to wade through. It will be perfectly all right—and it is no contradiction—to use what editors have given you (such as the footnotes at the bottom of the page or thumbing through copies of SparkNotes or No Fear Shakespeare). All I ask is that you jump up on your feet and try his words on for size before you do that. Think of it this way: 400 years from now an actor picking up a play by Neil LaBute or Suzan-Lori Parks will have to do research on *them,* too.

Consider this "research" process as *enrichment*, based on the words and the situations in a text you are already familiar with. It must not hamper in any way your human intuition or impulse, and the excitement and joy you experience—and thereby help *us* to experience!—when you simply say his words.

So, to answer the question of what you have read so far means for your acting, I offer the following summary:

1. Shakespeare's plays were meant to be performed, not merely read.
2. Shakespeare's words contain everything the audience—and *you*—need to know.
3. Shakespeare's plays are non-realistic but you must play them as *real to you.*
4. You are *telling* the story at the same time you are *living in* the story.
5. No "fourth wall" means you must always be alive on stage.
6. You must *share* the play with the entire audience.
7. Cue scripts help you to really listen, stay alert, and to be in the moment.

8. Play Shakespeare's words first, and *then* you may use research his actors didn't have.

Shakespeare has given you more to say and do than any other playwright that has ever lived. That is why I call him an actor's best friend forever. But to make all of this highfalutin stuff even simpler consider this: you are telling a story to someone you care about. What do *you* do to make sure they understand?

---

1 Best friend forever!
2 Sanford Meisner (1905–1997) was an American actor and acting teacher who established what is now known as the Meisner Technique, based on the "Reality of Doing" facilitated by his famous Repetition Exercise.
3 *The Tempest* was listed in the First Folio of 1623 as a comedy. Because of its elements of tragicomedy, combining buffoonish characters with dark themes of revenge against public figures while at the same time ending happily, since the Renaissance it has been more referred to by scholars as a romance.

Act Two

HOLDING UP MIRRORS

for anything so overdone is from the purpose of playing, whose end, both at the first and now, was and is, to hold, as 'twere, the mirror up to nature . . .

(Hamlet)

Shakespeare as a Cold Read

But masters, here are your parts, and I am to entreat you, request you and desire you, to con them by tomorrow night . . .

(Peter Quince to the rude mechanicals in
A Midsummer Night's Dream)

Think of this: you arrive at an audition where sides are provided. Perhaps you have been instructed by your teacher, or if you are already out of school and in New York City pounding the pavement, looking for work, perhaps you are being sent out by a theatrical agent and they have just gotten instructions from the casting director stating what role you are up for. Either way, all you know is that certain roles are being cast in a specific play and you are right for one of them. It may be you have already seen the director and casting people once; maybe you just did a prepared monologue for them. *If they liked you* they will direct you to the audition stage manager outside the door and tell you to ask for a specific side to read from, to hear how you might play a particular part. They tell you to look it over for a few minutes and then come back into the room later to read. This is a *cold* reading because you are, in effect, coming into it "cold"; you have not had the time to go over the script in advance and you have only the next few minutes to study it before you are to go back into the room and *do* something with it.

This is not far from what Shakespeare's actors might have faced after being handed their scroll. The exception of course is that today, in the cold-read scenario above, you are auditioning for a part in a play; in Shakespeare's time you would be getting ready to do a show *that day*! Talk about immediacy!

Because of the way Shakespeare's actors would have been handed their parts and because they might have had a performance of the play that very afternoon there would have been very little time for analysis. There was no time to ponder and ask: "Why am I saying this?" or, "What's my motivation?" It was sufficient you knew *that* you said it, that you *had* to say it because it was your job. To be fair you probably would have had at least some idea of the *type* of character you were playing; if you were a young boy your part might be Juliet. If you were a little older your role might have been Lady Macbeth. If you were Richard Burbage, the leading man of the company, you would have been cast as Hamlet, Will Kempe the character man would have played Falstaff or perhaps even Peter in *Romeo and Juliet* (pay close attention next time you see *Romeo and Juliet*; in a play that desperately needs lighter moments does not Peter get a lot of the laughs in the show?). Shakespeare's actors may have not wasted their time over the question of motivation because they knew that motivation would already be built into their lines. So yes, indeed you must know what you are speaking and why, even when the text is from the greatest playwright that ever lived.

When you first pick up unfamiliar Shakespeare text I ask that you not get nervous; I ask that you get energized. I ask that you think of it as an idyllic improvisation resulting in the opportunity for you to perform. Coming to the material "cold" is your big chance—for *excitement.* Suppose that the role *has never been played before,* until *now,* by *you?* Doing this will open up your performance for wonderful discovery, and by the way this is good advice no matter what kind of play you are acting in.

That's what this next section is about.

Lessons Introduction

Some of these lessons may be out of context; that's intentional. In putting all this together what I have also done, intentionally as well, is to leave out *footnotes.* Shakespeare's actors didn't have footnotes. I know the plays are heavily laden with archaic slang and cultural allusions, but the ideas are so universal you will eventually get past all that.

As you start, *do* them cold. Don't look for notes until later, after you have worked on the speeches for a while. I am going to bet that, more often than you might think, after simply following the clues Shakespeare has given you in the words—in the *sound* of the words—you won't be too far off what it all means.

When trying these improvs it is handy to have the speeches memorized but that is not crucial. *Just keep doing them.* Jump in, play, and imagine that you are telling a story to 3000 of your closest friends in broad daylight. Then do them all again and again, *acting* Shakespeare rather than *thinking* about acting Shakespeare. This is the best way "to hold, as 'twere, the mirror up to nature . . ."

Now, one more thing: the most important task of the actor is to deliver a performance that is truthful and clear, so clear that even a character's most fantastic, unbelievable actions can be made believable to an audience. This is true of course in the most realistic plays we see today, and it is just as true in classical theatre, especially the plays of William Shakespeare. These exercises are meant to help you reach the organic, fun, and, yes, *realistic* possibilities, through trial-and-error self-discovery, that can only come after every choice you can think of has been examined, whether good, bad, or—ready now—outrageous.

A performance that is only a voice-driven pronouncement of Shakespeare, as if the actor were trying to demonstrate how melodiously resonant their vocal instrument could be, cannot be believed. As an audience member I am moved to laugh or cry after listening to a *human being*, maybe like me, who just *happens* to be speaking soaring poetry, and speaking it in such a way that helps me to learn not only something about life, but maybe something about *myself*. Making Shakespeare's language *your own* is what makes his plays "classical." To me that is what it means to act Shakespeare. That is the kind of acting I want you to do.

Warm-up

Before you begin it is always a good idea to warm up your voice and body. Please, nothing too strenuous. Dress in loose-fitting clothing, whatever you can move around in. You can choose to do any physical warm-up you know, even the kind of stretches you might use to prepare for dance class or, yes, even before a workout at the gym, and you can even go through the kind of vocal scales you might do before singing an aria (you are, in fact, *singing* when you speak Shakespeare). In a pinch, you can limit your warm-up to your voice, concentrating on breath control and articulation. Loose and warm at least from the waist up. But again please: take it easy and *only do what you can*. Do not hurt yourself!

Remembering that you must always breathe normally, here are some warm-ups you can do:

- Head-rolling, from left to forward to right and back; then gradually a smooth gentle roll.
- Shoulder rolls, forward and back, arms loosely at your sides.
- Reaching up to ceiling, *genuinely* looking at what you are grasping for, as if you were crawling up the rungs of a ladder. Honestly try to catch that rung in your fingers.

- Stretch the ribcage, side to side. This is done by reaching as far as you can to one side, then to the other.
- Stand and *slowly* sink forward, bending over, to touch the floor, please bending your knees. Your hands should be able to touch the floor, but in any event don't push it at first; just go as far as you can go. Then slowly roll back up to standing. Imagine stacking each back vertebra on top of itself bone by bone, as if you were stacking wooden play blocks. From the bottom to full standing. The last thing that rises up into place should be your head upon your shoulders. This cannot be done too slowly. Then do it in reverse, slowly rolling down—head leading the way this time—and gradually fold down to where, with your knees bent (please!), your knuckles can touch the floor.
- Massage your face, inside the eye sockets, along the jaw line, and just under the cheekbones. Be rough on yourself as you knead the skin on your face. Remove your glasses or at least be careful around your eyes if you wear contact lenses.
- Stretch your mouth open wide, your eyes bulged wide open, making a "big face" and hold it for a beat. Then relax. Then do it several times.
- Scrunch your facial features inward as small as possible, as if you were a child pouting. Hold this pose for a beat, and then relax. Feel the gradual relaxing of your facial muscles. Then alternate between "big face" and "little face," back and forth, for a count of thousand one, thousand two, then switching.
- Stretch your tongue out as far as you can, like a happy dog. Allow yourself to feel the stretch in the muscles of your palate. Then, keeping your tongue out, try to speak as clearly as possible. It won't be possible, but it will begin to sharpen your tongue and lip articulation. If you know the words of the Shakespeare monologue—or *any* monologue—try to speak that, honestly *try* to act it.
- Slide your tongue inside your lips along your teeth, as if you are trying to get rid of peanut butter stuck there. Imagine

that the tip of your tongue is the bristle of a toothbrush and you are actually able to delve into every crevice of your teeth. Try to speak a line of text as you do this. It won't be possible but try to articulate the words as clearly as you can anyway.

- Blow air through your lips, once with allowing sound to come out, as well as once voiceless, simply air rushing out. *Try to see how much spit you can let fly.*
- Hang your tongue out and pant like a dog. Feel the pulse in your diaphragm. Just don't allow your shoulders to pop up; the only action you should feel is in the muscles of your stomach.
- Gently speak vowels out loud, A, E, I, O, U, rising in pitch, in ascending order and then descending order. Draw them out and see how many times you can do it on one breath. Then repeat, building up how long you can hold breath. This will help you increase your breath control capacity.
- Do singing warm-ups, the kind your voice teacher might take you through with a piano accompanist, including "Mee May Mah Moe Moo" ascending both up the scale and back down again. Of course you can do the standard "Do Ray Me Fa So La Tee Doh." Another one is "I'm hooommmee againnnn," once more going up in scale at the top of *home*. Again, as you rise in pitch, remember your teacher telling you not to let your shoulders rise up.
- Shake out your arms, legs, gently roll your head. You are ready to begin.

It takes great vocal energy to speak Shakespeare—and even to be a stage actor. Contemporary actors in training, partly out of shyness and perhaps out of today's infatuation with "doing film," have the habit of mumbling, of being imprecise when speaking, of allowing themselves to lose energy at the end of a line. When told about this, what the student will often do is burst forth with a great deal of energy at the *beginning* of the line, but because of insufficient breath control they gradually lose air at the end and peter out like a balloon collapsing. If you err in too much energy it is best to do so at the *end* of the line. This will do two things: first it will help you to sense the building momentum in a speech, and second it will help you immeasurably with *articulation*. One of the best ways to improve your articulation and diction *at once* is to simply hit the consonants; consonants are a stage actor's—or any actor's—best friend. Believe it or not this will also help you with *projection*; it is easier for the audience ear if they can make out clearly what you say at the end of a line, those Ts, Ds, Ks, Gs, etc. The additional handy byproduct of this is that using the ends of words as a help for projection will prevent you from suddenly shouting after you have been told that you cannot be heard from the back of the house. Every stage actor should, if they do nothing else before a performance, warm up and practice hitting the consonants hard. We in this country are lazy at this and it may take some time to get used to exerting the extra effort, but it will improve your vocal instrument no matter what kind of acting you do. Honest.

Lesson 1: Doing

Things won are done; joy's soul lies in the doing.
(Troilus and Cressida)

These lessons can be done in a wide variety of ways and settings, either by yourself or with a partner or friends or in the classroom. They require no special materials other than Shakespeare's words, and *you*.

Exercise 1: Howl

In Act V, Scene 5, the final scene of Shakespeare's tragedy *King Lear*, the old king wanders on stage, carrying the dead body of his youngest—and dearest—daughter. It is one of the most famous scenes in a canon overflowing with famous scenes. The old man's first words are, simply:

Howl, howl, howl, howl!

He has more to say in what is actually a fairly short speech. But don't worry about that yet. This exercise, like most of them, can be done in a classroom or even—if you have understanding neighbors—in your apartment. As part of this first improvisation what I want you to do is this: say these four words aloud—*Howl, howl, howl, howl*—in the following ways:

1. Say each word one at a time, slowly. Say each word drawing out the sound so that you are making them into more syllables; for instance, how-el, h–o–ow–e–ell–uh. Do this with each of the words. Don't worry about understandability.
2. Say each word at the top of your voice.
3. Say each word in your most quiet voice (notice I do not say *whisper*: whispering is actually raspy for your voice).
4. Say each word rapidly, in a fast staccato.
5. Say each word very slowly, legato.
6. Say them doing all of these things in a series of sentences, making a veritable monologue out of just these four words.
7. Say them with your arms outstretched, far out in front of you, as if you were carrying the limp body of Cordelia in your arms. *Really* reach out forward; don't be afraid of being melodramatic.
8. Say them all of these ways and then collapse onto the floor, exhausted, after carrying her on stage. Then get up, and do the entire speech, clean, without the adjustments.

You don't need to be concerned with acting or emotion. You only have to speak these four words out loud, in all of the ways above and as many other ways you can think of. Do it over and over again before you attempt the rest of the speech.

Why, you might ask? I have a thought. Shakespeare's plays—in fact all plays, when you really get down to it—are about *size*, about problems people have to deal with that are heavy and great—even if those problems are *wonderful*, you know? How awesome is the task of getting up the gumption to ask someone to marry you? And then—how much greater once they have said *yes*? This exercise is not only about text that is sorrowful or tragic—it is about coming into touch with needs that are so huge to us we have no way—or *words*—to express them. Sometimes, my friends, actors find it hard to make the "big choice." You know what I mean: to go over the top, to overdo, to "chew the scenery," out of fear of perhaps looking foolish in front of peers, or because of doing something wrong. Dear ones, let me tell you: in training, as long as you do no harm to yourself or another soul you can *do no wrong*. If you are loud, if you lose your place in a script, if you fall down, if you don't know what you are doing, if you are uncertain as the class looks on you—*so what*?

This first item is about helping you, at least eventually, to get there, to go to that fearful place and trust that you will be all right. Think of it this way: if you are trying for a career as an actor, what greater risk and threat of failure can there possibly be than *that*?

The other thing that it's about is guiding you, introducing you, to the sound and shape and scope of Shakespeare's words, his, yes, *outrageous* words and the outrageous situations that have caused his characters to need to say them.

Don't worry. Everything will be all right. Let's go.

Exercise 2: Sing

Yes I said it. *Sing*. In Act III, Scene 4 of Shakespeare's great comedy *Twelfth Night*, the doltish Puritan Malvolio has just convinced himself that his mistress, Olivia, is in love with him. Once alone he has a long speech to reassure himself of this, but he begins the speech with but two words:

O, ho!

I want you to take these two words and, in the same way that you played and explored and discovered with Exercise 1, I want you to *sing* these two words, over and over and over again. Sing as if you are actually singing a song, not through articulating and shaping the words. Do you need to be able to sing? Of course not! This fact has not stopped anyone who, by the course of human events, was *moved* to sing. Have you ever been moved to sing? When you are by yourself, certain that you are alone, have you ever hummed a little tune, a song you know or like, have you ever tried to sing along while driving and listening to the radio or shampooing your hair in the shower? Have you? Out of love of country have you ever mumbled—poorly—the national anthem at a ball game? Or a hymn in church? Can you think of any human personal event in your past when you have felt compelled to emit a tuneful melody, to express some weighty moment of whimsy and delight?

Or, perhaps more importantly, are you willing to *imagine* feeling so moved?

That's what this improv is about. You don't have to be able to sing. If you can, great; enjoy making lovely melodic sound. If not, just as great! Sing badly out loud, to the top of your voice! If you can't think of or make up a tune, use "Happy Birthday!" It is no less great, because you are living a personal human moment in time when a thing is done for no other reason than to express reverence, or *happiness.*

Now, it is no mistake that these first items have to do with making sounds to express either extreme (outrageous) sorrow or exultation. But you can twist them around and do the opposite with each. You can choose to sing "Howl!" or cry out "O ho!" You can even find single words or a very short sentence from Shakespeare's other plays and play the exercise using them. How about Juliet's "Come, vial"? Or Hamlet's "O, vengeance"?

Exercise 3: Don't Think About It

This one is very simple. It asks you to get up onto your feet, reading and performing Shakespeare out loud, without being hamstrung by the contemporary notion of motivation. It is not that motivation is unimportant; that will come later. This just gets you into the habit of performing and memorizing *first*, and relying upon the *text* to tell you what your character's motivation is.

Pick up a Shakespeare monologue. It can be blank verse or prose.

How about trying this one by Dromio of Ephesus from *The Comedy of Errors* (Act I, Scene 2):

> Return'd so soon! rather approach'd too late:
> The capon burns, the pig falls from the spit,
> The clock hath strucken twelve upon the bell;
> My mistress made it one upon my cheek:
> She is so hot because the meat is cold;
> The meat is cold because you come not home;
> You come not home because you have no stomach;
> You have no stomach having broke your fast;
> But we that know what 'tis to fast and pray
> Are penitent for your default to-day.

Just get on your feet and start reading aloud. Don't attempt to analyze or try to understand the arcane phrases or contractions or made-up words. For this exercise you do not even have to have it memorized. Just do it. *Act* it. *Right now!*

Do this:

1. Position yourself in the middle of the room, establishing imaginary "audience" left, center, and right of you.
2. Position far imaginary galleries of people *up high* out in front of you—say the top of the ceiling over your head—and down below at the foot of the stage—toward the groundlings—at your feet.
3. Now go! *Tell the story*. If you are not sure, tell what you *think* the story is.

After doing this check yourself:

- Was it a disaster of confusion?
- Did you eventually get "into" it?
- Did you eventually sense not only the *sound* but also the *shape* of the words?
- Did concentrating on the sound and shape of the words, both arcane contracted and made up, help you in any way?
- Did *every* word have meaning? Or not?
- Did you ever sense when *one* word *seemed* to have more meaning than another?
- Did the *active verbs* help you along the way?
- Did the end of the *sentences* help you along the way?
- Did the end of the *speech* help you along the way?

Consider these aspects. The

sound of the words
shape of the words
active verb
end of each *sentence*
end of the *speech*.

Now do it again. And again. *Then* you may look over the footnotes. For fun you might play a little game to see if you got close to the meaning. But either way after checking the notes *do it again*. And check yourself *again*. What do you think of your performance after that? How did knowledge of the words you did not understand before affect your performance? Is it *possible*, when you did it for the first time, that not knowing what the words meant could have somehow injected something, an extra energy, an extra *oomph*, into your performance? Think about it. Then pick up another speech and do the improv all over again.

One more thing: don't be at all surprised if, at the end of this exercise, you discover that you have nearly *memorized* the monologue!

Exercise 4: Hop, Kneel, Crawl, and Hug!

At a moment in the speech—pick one which could make sense; if it does not, do it anyway!—do one of these actions: hop in place, bow down to the floor, crawl about the floor, or hug your sides in vigorous celebration or complaint. It makes no matter if this is done suddenly and out of place (under stress we do things that are out of place); simply concentrate on what, if anything, the act of doing these things does to the speech and your understanding of the character's needs and desires. If they are happy, could not all of them fit in? If sad, why not all of them yet again?

Practice it with this speech of Caliban, from *The Tempest* (Act I, Scene 2):

> I must eat my dinner.
> This island's mine, by Sycorax my mother,
> Which thou takest from me. When thou camest first,
> Thou strokedst me and madest much of me, wouldst give me
> Water with berries in't, and teach me how
> To name the bigger light, and how the less,
> That burn by day and night: and then I loved thee
> And show'd thee all the qualities o' the isle,
> The fresh springs, brine-pits, barren place and fertile:
> Cursed be I that did so! All the charms
> Of Sycorax, toads, beetles, bats, light on you!
> For I am all the subjects that you have,
> Which first was mine own king: and here you sty me
> In this hard rock, whiles you do keep from me
> The rest' the island.

Are there any moments when it seems to you appropriate that Caliban, who is speaking to his master Prospero, might actually need to hop? Or kneel? Or crawl? Or hug? To hop out of a fit of aggression, then kneel in apology, then crawl and hug out of an attempt to gain favor? What do either of these efforts do to the sound of the words, your understanding of the words, and your performance of the words? What might they do to any speech, such as—yes I know it's crazy—Hamlet's "O what a rogue and peasant slave am I"?

Exercise 5: Wrestle, Kick, Speak!

This lesson is to energize your body as well as voice before you begin to speak, to practice the drive and energy that is *expectant* upon every Shakespearean cue because you are forced to listen to every word. *Remember that this applies as much to speeches that are comedic and happy as well as to dramatic tragic speeches.*

Perform the following actions in *order*, and then start the speech:

- *Wrestle*

This can be physically on the floor or standing; begin first with simply the actual physical action, but also think of wrestling in terms of *emotional need* as well as a bodily altercation with an imaginary opponent. It is a struggle with a problem that forces you to react and do something about it. For instance: a "give me five" hand slap after some great triumph or a violent fist pump at some disappointment.

If you find that you are unable to imagine the forceful resistance that an actual person might present you can add objects such as a pillow, or a large rubber ball, a towel, anything that you can actually get your hands on to make it more tangible for yourself.

- *Kick* (if a dramatic speech) or *dance* (if a comedic one)

A physical action, whether it will solve the problem or not, out of a desire to do at least *something*. Kick at some foe, some problem, at *some* imagined enemy. Dance for joy, with a make-believe partner.

- *Speak* (start the monologue or the scene)

Finally you are forced to speak out loud in order to solve your problem. Allow the previous physical actions to affect your performance.

Try it with this speech of Malvolio from *Twelfth Night*:

> Daylight and champian discovers not more: this is open. I will be proud, I will read politic authors, I will baffle Sir Toby, I will wash off gross acquaintance, I will be point-devise the very man. I do not now fool myself, to let imagination jade me; for every reason excites to this, that my lady loves me. She did commend my yellow stockings of late, she did praise my leg being cross-gartered; and in this she manifests herself to my love, and with a kind of injunction drives me to these habits of her liking. I thank my stars I am happy. I will be strange, stout, in yellow stockings, and cross-gartered, even with the swiftness of putting on. Jove and my stars be praised!

This speech is from Act II, Scene 5. As an adjustment try the three efforts before each *line*.

Exercise 6: You Are Being Chased

This works best when memorized, but don't let not knowing the words ever stop you. Use any struggle for words you can't remember *to drive your need to speak*. Perform the speech, at all times, with the need to *get away* from some*one* or some*thing*. You simply *cannot* exit the room! All you can play is the need to *escape*. After every line with a pause or stop in the text (such as a period, comma, colon, or semi-colon), run to a different place on the stage or in the room, to duck, cower, and hide. Use any piece of furniture around you as cover. Depending upon the size of the theater you can even leap out into the house and scamper up and down the aisles. The only rule is you may not exit the space. *Then*, back on stage, do the monologue again, even if out of breath, *without* the rushing away to hide. Are you energized? Are you possessed with an outrageous need to speak? To communicate? Then do it again. And still again.

Try it with this speech of Isabella, from *Measure for Measure*, at the end of Act II, Scene 4:

> To whom should I complain? Did I tell this,
> Who would believe me? O perilous mouths,
> That bear in them one and the self-same tongue,
> Either of condemnation or approof;
> Bidding the law make court'sy to their will:
> Hooking both right and wrong to the appetite,
> To follow as it draws! I'll to my brother:
> Though he hath fallen by promptness of the blood,
> Yet hath he in him such a mind of honour.
> That, had he twenty heads to tender down
> On twenty bloody blocks, he'ld yield them up,
> Before his sister should her body stoop
> To such abhorr'd pollution.
> Then, Isabel, live chaste, and, brother, die:
> More than our brother is our chastity.
> I'll tell him yet of Angelo's request,
> And fit his mind to death, for his soul's rest.

This exercise is also about beats and changing thoughts and action. In effect, as you dash about the room, driven by being chased, *you* are in fact chasing *after* the next need in your desire to communicate. Consider this improv a companion to Exercise 7, which follows below.

Exercise 7: Every Line is a New Discovery

This is to help you feel how active and "in the moment" the desire to fight for an answer can be. At first it is quite all right to use the actual printed text to keep your place. Try this:

- Stand and speak the speech out loud.
- Play the beginning of every new line (new line meaning punctuation; from full end stop with a period), as a *new discovery*, not thought of before.
- Then play every new discovery with a new *reaction*.
- As an adjustment you can help with this by shouting "Ah ha!" before each line.
- With every new line and new discovery walk in a completely new *direction*, "Ah ha!" carrying you forth.
- As you draw near the end of the speech allow your voice to rise in pitch and your moves to lift you off your feet; i.e., skip or jump or lunge. Go ahead and allow a final, loudest pronouncement of "Ah ha!" to punctuate your ending discovery.

Do the speech again, immediately, *without* the movement, keeping each discovery. Play the speech punctuation to punctuation, so that you do not fall into the habit of stopping at the end of an unbroken line. Rather than a stop that might be suggested by "Ah ha!" let that discovery drive you to the *next* discovery, and the next and then the next, etc. *Let what your character learns drive the speech.* You will discover that this improv is also about *changing beats*, i.e., discovering one new *thought* after another.

Exercise 8: **Become *the Words***

When telling a story which you want to make vivid to the listener, don't you get up and act out some of the crazy images and things that happen in your tale? Does it not help your listener to "get into" the story if you demonstrate to them what you are talking about by physically seeming to *become* those images? Yes, you are ahead of me; a game of *charades*. To play with this notion you can choose any of Shakespeare's monologues. For this exercise listed here is Mercutio's long monologue from *Romeo and Juliet*. You are free to use sounds as well to help you become the objects of the monologue.

The Queen Mab Speech

This famous speech works quite well when becoming the words. It has been possibly the very reason—along with swordplay—to play the role of Mercutio. Critics do not agree on what it means; they only accept that it can be a tour de force—as well as a very bear—for an actor to assail. I hear the confusion, but I should like to respectfully say that for actors such academic worry is beside the point; actors about to do a show should ditch scholarly mumbo-jumbo and just *have fun.* So try it out and put your own stamp on it, and leave scholarship behind to puzzle over itself in an ivory tower (is my agenda seeping out?). And, ladies, you try it, too; Mercutio has been played by women. For this exercise it is okay to read the play first if you like (though by now you know why I am not requiring you to do that), and then get busy. Where helpful check the iambic pentameter meter, but don't let that bog you down. The more you work on Shakespeare speeches the more you will probably find a version that is in prose instead of verse, which you will likely begin to see thanks to persnickety disparate editors. But I think Shakespeare himself would be happiest if you just simply *do it.* Don't worry about if it is "right." What's right? It can always change. The entire speech is listed in the "Practice Speeches" appendix in the back of this book, so here is just a portion of it for you to think about. To help you, allow me to suggest a bit of my own interpretation, which I have tried to take from the story of the play itself. Maybe these thoughts will guide you through this glorious unwieldy speech. If I were to try to guess what it is about, I would say that one possibility is, "Boy, doesn't love make us do crazy stuff!" But here, in the form of given circumstances, is what I think you can rely on from the play itself:

1. Mercutio has a way with words.
2. Mercutio loves to hear himself talk.
3. Mercutio is always teasing his dear friend Romeo because Romeo is constantly lovesick.

4. My last suggestion is: don't play the Shakespeare scholar: play *a brilliant man making fun of his best friend!*

Here are a few active verbs you can use to play the scene. Remember that each of these, in the context of the scene, involves Mercutio playing *to* and *with* Romeo, so that you would use the verb "make fun of" in the context of doing it *to* your partner (Romeo).

> Ridicule
> Tease
> Laugh at
> Woo
> Celebrate
> Soothe

The images below, in **bold** type, are examples of what you can seize upon from the speech to "become" in your performance. For the hundredth time, as you read them *don't allow not knowing what they mean to prevent you from acting*; do what the *sound* and *energy* of these words suggest to *you*. You'll find the true meaning in research later.

> She is the **fairies' midwife**, and she comes
> In shape no bigger than an **agate-stone**
> On the fore-finger of an **alderman**,
> Drawn with a team of little **atomies** . . .
> Her wagon-spokes made of **long spiders' legs**,
> The cover of the **wings of grasshoppers**,
> The traces of the **smallest spider's web**,
> The **collars** of the **moonshine's watery beams**,
> Her **whip** of **cricket's bone**, the **lash of film**,
> Her **wagoner** a small **grey-coated gnat** . . ., etc., etc.

Try everything that comes to your mind, driven by the sound, shape, length, and weight of the words. How would you actually become an "atomie"? Or an agate-stone? What would your body do to replicate spider's legs, or grasshopper wings, a spider's web, etc.? Don't worry one whit about context or meaning. The point is to play like a child on the playground. Then, as always, do the speech *without* these gyrations and see what happens to you and your understanding of what Mercutio is trying to tell the audience about his friend Romeo! The performance must not be about doing charades. You will not act out every single gesture and movement; what you want to retain is the sense and essence of what the *desire to communicate* causes a human being to do!

Variation: Let the Class Choose What You Become

As a variation on the exercise, try it in class with your fellow actors, or if you are at a party and folks are willing, try it there as a fun game. Teacher, have everyone write down on a piece of paper their best choice of object or action—animals, weather, food, places, things, etc. Then gather them up and swirl them around in a bowl or hat. Pick one out and do it! Act the speech that way! Yet another variation is to have people from the group shout their choice out loud, one after the other, shotgun fashion, until all of their choices are performed!

Lesson 2: Verse

Hang there, my verse, in witness of my love.
                                                            (*As You Like It*)

All right. You are up on your feet and you have started reading out loud. Continue to explore every particle of Shakespeare's words; every syllable and sound. You just might discover that you are getting closer not only to what those words mean, but how using them—without resorting to Stanislavskian "sense memory" of your dead dog or unrequited love—will actually help you start to *feel* something.

Exercise 9: Write It in Prose

Sometimes when actors first read Shakespearean blank verse aloud they have a tendency to want to stop at the end of the line, even if there is no visible stop at the end of it. To help with this I provide this exercise. Take your blank verse speech and either hand-write or type it out, converting it into *prose*. Un-capitalize the beginning of lines on the left-hand side of the page that are capitalized if they are not following a period. Using Helena's speech from *A Midsummer Night's Dream* from the "Practice Speeches" appendix, I have written it out in the way you might find more familiar. I have added **bold** type to highlight the previous capitalized letters that you are to change to lower case, but make sure that it does not cause you to emphasize them any more than you normally would.

> How happy some o'er other some can be! Through Athens I am thought as fair as she. But what of that? Demetrius thinks not so; **h**e will not know what all but he do know: **a**nd as he errs, doting on Hermia's eyes, **s**o I, admiring of his qualities. Things base and vile, holding no quantity, **l**ove can transpose to form and dignity: love looks not with the eyes, but with the mind; **a**nd therefore is wing'd Cupid painted blind: **n**or hath Love's mind of any judgment taste; **w**ings and no eyes figure unheedy haste: **a**nd therefore is Love said to be a child, **b**ecause in choice he is so oft beguiled. As waggish boys in game themselves forswear, **s**o the boy Love is perjured everywhere: **f**or ere Demetrius look'd on Hermia's eyne, **h**e hail'd down oaths that he was only mine; **a**nd when this hail some heat from Hermia felt, **s**o he dissolved, and showers of oaths did melt. I will go tell him of fair Hermia's flight: **t**hen to the wood will he tomorrow night **p**ursue her; and for this intelligence **i**f I have thanks, it is a dear expense: **b**ut herein mean I to enrich my pain, **t**o have his sight thither and back again.

Now read aloud. Be certain to strictly follow the *new* "punctuation" your rewrite has created. "Speak the speech as I pronounced it to you . . ." Go!

Then check yourself:

- Did the speech make more sense to you?
- Did it flow more "naturally"?
- Does it sound more "conversational"?
- Did you sense clearer meaning by its end?

Consider these questions and read aloud again. And again.

Exercise 10: Tear the Words!

This wild improvisation is based on Julia's "kind Julia / unkind Julia" speech from *The Two Gentlemen of Verona*. It's a bit crazy but that's what you want to help you stay alert and listening and to embrace the reckless play of memorizing in mere hours for a Shakespearean performance in front of 3000 people.

Take an iambic pentameter speech, perhaps Julia's, or you might pick the Prologue from *Henry V* spoken by the Chorus:

> O for a Muse of fire, that would ascend
> The brightest heaven of invention,
> A kingdom for a stage, princes to act
> And monarchs to behold the swelling scene!
> Then should the warlike Harry, like himself,
> Assume the port of Mars; and at his heels,
> Leash'd in like hounds, should famine, sword and fire
> Crouch for employment. But pardon, and gentles all,
> The flat unraised spirits that have dared
> On this unworthy scaffold to bring forth
> So great an object: can this cockpit hold
> The vasty fields of France? Or may we cram
> Within this wooden O the very casques
> That did affright the air at Agincourt?

> O, pardon! since a crooked figure may
> Attest in little place a million;
> And let us, ciphers to this great accompt,
> On your imaginary forces work.
> Suppose within the girdle of these walls
> Are now confined two mighty monarchies,
> Whose high upreared and abutting fronts
> The perilous narrow ocean parts asunder:
> Piece out our imperfections with your thoughts;
> Into a thousand parts divide on man,
> And make imaginary puissance;
> Think when we talk of horses, that you see them
> Printing their proud hoofs i' the receiving earth;
> For 'tis your thoughts that now must deck our kings,
> Carry them here and there; jumping o'er times,
> Turning the accomplishment of many years
> Into an hour-glass: for the which supply,
> Admit me Chorus to this history;
> Who prologue-like your humble patience pray,
> Gently to hear, kindly to judge, our play.

Now do this:

- Print it out on a piece of paper with a lot of space between each line, a double space minimum but it can even be triple space. Use a font size of 16 or 18 or even greater.
- Then tear all of the lines on the page into *single, one-line strips.*
- Next toss the strips up into the air! Scatter them about the floor!
- And then—you guessed it—scurry about the floor, picking up one strip after the other after the other, and *act them!*

Go quickly, grabbing up a strip and speaking it, then as fast as you can snatching up the next piece, reading it and then the other, and the other, until you have all of the torn strips in your hands. Then toss them up into the air and do it all again.

Exercise 11: Hang Your Verse

For this exercise it is handy—though you can use any blank verse speech you wish—to choose Orlando's words that open Act III, Scene 2 from *As You Like It*:

> Hang there, my verse, in witness of my love:
> And thou, thrice-crowned queen of night, survey
> With thy chaste eye, from thy pale sphere above,
> Thy huntress' name that my full life doth sway.
> O Rosalind! these trees shall be my books
> And in their barks my thoughts I'll character;
> That every eye which in this forest looks
> Shall see thy virtue witness'd everywhere.
> Run, run, Orlando; carve on every tree
> The fair, the chaste and unexpressive she.

This continues the "Tear the Word" exercise, but it is inspired by Orlando's scene. This may work best in the classroom where you have a host of classmates who can help, but with a little effort you can do it by yourself. With this improv I present you with two ways to do it:

1. *Do it un-memorized*

This will require a bit of preparation, but it can help you to be impulsive and in the moment. Allow any leaning forward out of trying to read the paper to energize you.

- To get started, begin with the first two lines of the speech. Write *one word each* in order on 8½ by 11 inch pieces of paper. Use as many pieces of paper as words to speak. Make the letters very large, fill the page so that the word is big enough to be seen from a distance. You must be able to read them perhaps from an estimate of the front row of the audience to you on the stage down center; think 10 or 15 feet (it will depend upon your theater space).

- Set up, in order, each placard you have created. Set them in an easy-to-see row from left to right. Standing them in chairs (not unlike audience members) is nice but if you have only a few chairs you can place two (or more) placards in a single chair at a time. Of course if you are doing this in class you can have your classmates hold the pieces of paper up for you.
- *Do* the speech! Beginning at your left, then rushing to the next placard, then the next, and the next. You are performing the speech one word at a time but as quickly and fluidly as possible. Play the scene!

2. *Do it memorized*

This is perhaps the handiest way, as it does not require the pieces of paper or even the seats in the theater or classroom space. Instead of using those objects do this:

- With each image/verse, glance quickly at a point in the room. It can be:
  - At the ceiling
  - At the window
  - At the floor
  - At your right corner
  - At your left corner
  - At the doorway
  - At the EXIT sign
  - If in a classroom or theater with classmates, dart glances at each of *them*, randomly, not from one directly to the other, so that you can feel the manic haste to get your verse posted on the "tree limbs." You can do this exercise with any Shakespearean text in which the character has a list of things to speak about.

  Then afterward, at the end, check yourself:
  - Are you out of breath?
  - Are you energized?

- Have you made sense of the text?
- Have you felt an outrageous *need to communicate?*

Write out the rest of the speech and do it the same way. Then do the speech *without* the placards!

Exercise 12: Verb to Verb

In Shakespeare playing the words is also about playing the verbs, the active verbs. In Lesson 4, which is devoted to emotion, we do this in a different way. But first you want to find the character's action in speaking, and Shakespeare helps you do this through his use of verbs. Verbs are among the first clues you will rely upon when trying to make sense of the text. Try this, using the Chorus from *Romeo and Juliet* (listed among the "Practice Speeches" in the appendix). Highlight each verb you can find, and then speak each one, performing those verbs (in **bold** below) alone as the speech.

> Two households, both alike in dignity,
> In fair Verona, where we **lay** our scene,
> From ancient grudge **break** to new mutiny,
> Where civil blood **makes** civil hands unclean.
> From forth the fatal loins of these two foes
> A pair of star-**cross'd** lovers **take** their life;
> Whose misadventured piteous **overthows**
> **Do** with their death **bury** their parents' strife.
> The fearful passage of their death-**mark'd** love,
> And the continuance of their parents' rage,
> Which, but their children's end, nought could **remove**,
> Is now the two hours' traffic of our stage;
> The which if you with patient ears **attend**,
> What here shall **miss**, our **toil** shall **strive** to **mend**.

Then play the speech as if it were made up of *only* the verbs:

> lay,
> break, mutiny

makes
take
overthrows
do
bury
remove
attend
toil, strive, mend

Then do the entire speech, and check yourself for new discoveries as you have emphasized and over-emphasized the verbs, and do it again with another speech. This exercise is not unlike "*Become* the Words"; a verb is an action and calls upon you to *do* something. To speak is to do. As you play the lesson see what it feels like to physically perform the verb. It may be that it is not unlike the system of Laban or Viewpoints, both good for helping actors to physicalize as a way to clarify text. As always, don't be afraid to *over*do. Then perform the speech without the gestures and see how they inform your delivery.

Lesson 3: Sound

Mark how one string, sweet husband to another,
Strikes each in each by mutual ordering.
(*Sonnet 8.9–10*)

Shakespeare is the master, I might argue perhaps even the creator, of onomatopoeia. Onomatopoeia is defined as "a word that sounds like what it means or imitates the sound of a thing." Shakespeare created words that do this. This lesson is initially for the prose speech that contains made-up, hard-to-understand words that you have not yet studied notes for, but it will work with any of the more difficult verse texts as well.

ACT TWO: HOLDING UP MIRRORS

Exercise 13: Gobbledygook

Do this: every time you come to a word that you don't understand, simply make up *anything* to say! What you make up doesn't need to have any reason, sense or meaning, and no association whatsoever to the text. What it must have is the *need to keep you talking*, trying to find the word you will say next. Continuing the fight is more important than the words you come up with. Keep going, keep clamoring for any random thing that comes to your mind to say. Replace the words with made-up ones of your own, and they don't even have to be words. They can even be sounds, vowels, moaning and groaning. A good choice to use from the "Practice Speeches" is this Master Ford speech below from *The Merry Wives of Windsor*. Here is some of what it might look like. **Bold** type is where I have injected my own crazy substitute words:

> What a damned **popcorn** rascal is this! My heart is ready to crack with impatience. Who says this is improvident jealousy? My wife hath sent to him; the hour is fixed; the match is made . . . Terms! Names! **Ooga-booga** sounds well; **Bozo**, well; **Skippy**, well; yet they are devils' additions, the names of fiends: but **Airplane! Coatrack!—Bloomers**! The devil himself hath not such a name . . . I will rather trust a **baseball** with my butter, Parson Hugh the Welshman with my cheese, an Irishman with my **smoothie** bottle . . . I will about it; better three hours too soon than a minute too late. **Argh! Skoobie-doo! Tree truck! Bazzfazz!**

Exercise 14: "Duh, Hell-oh, F—k!"

In the same way that we say, "Duh-uhh?" or "Hello—*ooh!*" or the violence with which we hit the "k" when we drop the F-bomb, so the language of Shakespeare's words can do the same thing. For example, when we say to someone "Duh—*uhh*" with a sloping, up and down inflection, we might be trying to tell them, "You are stupid not to understand me." If we say, "Hell-*oh-ohh!*" with the same drawn-out twang, we're saying, "*Listen* to what I've been saying, you idiot!" We certainly do this in the foul language we (some of us) use, including "S—t!" or "Dammit!" The F-word is particularly descriptive when uttering extreme displeasure because of the consonants; notice how hard we strike the plosive "k" sound; the more egregious the event the harder we hammer it, right? And yes "plosive" does indicate *exploding*. In fact this is true when pounding all of the consonants—remember they are your best friend.

The same urge can be realized when in your vocal warm-ups you stretch the words into as many syllables you can make. In the *Playing Shakespeare* series as taught by John Barton, using the word "Time," it is explored how many syllables "time" can be made into, such as "T-ah-yy-i-eee-u-mm." The reason for this is not for the sake of vocal practice; it is rather to aid the actor in remembering—and rediscovering—the fact that we speak this way as *a means to communicate a need,* every day of our lives. This way the words are elongated or contracted because of human need in an outrageous situation caused by love rather than out of a desire to be "Shakespearean." Below are a few words used by Shakespeare you can use for practice. See how long and exaggerated you can make them sound:

Aye
Assay
Nay
O
Foul
Prey
Crown
Seems
Alone

The same can be practiced with sharply striking the consonants. Hit them very hard:

Gallop
Likest
Behold
Rank
Neglect
Bloody
Deed
Black
Dagger
Blackguard
Beweep
Boot
Hit
Fit

Lesson 4: Emotion

"O Peace!" quoth Lucrece: if it should be told,
The repetition cannot make it less;
For more it is than I can well express;
And that deep torture may be called a hell,
When more is felt than one hath power to tell.
(The Rape of Lucrece, 1284–1288)

The playing of emotion can prove to be the most daunting task for an actor, no matter what kind of play they are working on. Plays are ultimately about emotion, about—here it comes—human beings caught up in outrageous situations caused by love, and though plays do not—or ought not—require characters to wail and cry for three hours (as some mistakenly think is required of Greek tragedy), before the curtain comes down characters must, at least at some point, display to the audience what can be believed to be genuine human feeling; they must show emotion. Through training and experience actors will find their own path to best accomplish this, but at least in the plays of William Shakespeare you have been provided with clues to get there. These clues, of course, are the words, and this lesson offers a few improvisations to help you along the way.

If you look at Shakespeare's great emotional speeches you will find that many of them are very long, perhaps 40, 50, 60 lines of blank verse, or nearly a page of prose. Because they are so long, these speeches unfortunately can be among the first lines cut (or at least edited) when a director has to take a red pencil to a script to get the run-time of the performance down to less than three hours. Yes, it is necessary to make cuts to the script, but such editing must always be done with consummate skill, for it is in the very length of these speeches—the involved, extensive, exhaustive avalanche of words—that Shakespeare is helping his actors *build* to the emotion required of a tragic moment in the play.

Exercise 15: In-Motion, Not E-Motion

Study this speech below of Marcus Andronicus, from *Titus Andronicus* (Act II, Scene 4). Try reading it out loud. Don't try to *feel* it, at least not yet. Concentrate rather on the shape and sound of the consonants and the vowels, and on *telling the story* of the speech. After you are finished, having formed and shaped and breathed every word of the speech and strove to impart the story, is it possible that you might actually be *tired*?

This is a sign of the beginning of emotion.

To help you I have highlighted in **bold** type all of the verbs. In addition I have *italicized* names/references that might be strange to you.

> Who is this? My niece, that **flies** away so fast!
> Cousin, a word; where is your husband?
> If I do **dream**, would all my wealth would **wake** me!
> If I do **wake**, some planet **strike** me down,

ACT TWO: HOLDING UP MIRRORS

That I may **slumber** in eternal sleep!
Speak, gentle niece, what stern ungentle hands
Have **lopp'd** and **hew'd** and made thy body bare
Of her two branches, those sweet ornaments,
Whose **circling** shadows kings have **sought** to **sleep** in,
And might not **gain** so great a happiness
As have thy love? Why **dost** not **speak** to me?
Alas, a crimson river of warm blood,
Like to a bubbling fountain **stirr'd** with wind,
Doth **rise** and **fall** between thy rosèd lips,
Coming and **going** with thy honey breath.
But, sure, some *Tereus* hath **deflowered** thee,
And, lest thou shouldst **detect** him, **cut** thy tongue.
Ah, now thou **turn'st** away thy face for shame!
And, notwithstanding all this loss of blood,
As from a conduit with three **issuing** spouts,
Yet do thy cheeks look red as *Titan*'s face
Blushing to be encountered with a cloud.
Shall I **speak** for thee? shall I **say** 'tis so?
O, that I knew thy heart; and knew the beast,
That I might **rail** at him, to ease my mind!
Sorrow **concealed,** like an oven **stopp'd,**
Doth **burn** the heart to cinders where it is.
Fair *Philomela*, she but **lost** her tongue,
And in a tedious sampler **sew'd** her mind:
But, lovely niece, that mean is **cut** from thee;
A craftier *Tereus*, cousin, hast thou **met,**
And he hath **cut** those pretty fingers off,
That could have better **sew'd** than *Philomel*.
O, had the monster seen those lily hands
Tremble, like aspen-leaves, upon a lute,
And **make** the silken strings **delight** to **kiss** them,
He would not then have **touch'd** them for his life!
Or, had he **heard** the heavenly harmony
Which that sweet tongue hath **made,**
He would have **dropp'd** his knife, and **fell** asleep

As *Cerberus* at the *Thracian* poet's feet.
Come, let us **go**, and **make** thy father blind;
For such a sight will **blind** a father's eye:
One hour's storm will **drown** the fragrant meads;
What **will** whole months of tears thy father's eyes?
Do not **draw** back, for we will **mourn** with thee
O, could our mourning **ease** thy misery!

Yes, the speech is long. *Very* long.

But you might well discover that the actual length of the monologue must be long because Marcus's *grief* is long. Think of senseless tragedy in our society and world today, with sudden undeserved acts of terrorism, violence, and murder or senseless accidents that take the lives of undeserving innocents. Are not those who suffer or witness such horror given to crying aloud, "Why, why, *why*?" Some of them might even be compelled to deliver long, arduous speeches, as if to anyone who will listen, out of the need to unburden themselves, purge themselves, and struggle to somehow make sense of the insensible. Are not these speeches made long in fact because the speaker is struggling to find an *answer,* and they keep talking because the words that come to them are not enough to describe the depth of their despair? You might say that Marcus Andronicus is begging the *audience* for such an answer, and that is what makes his monologue emotional, and what helps the actor playing the scene to play it.

Perhaps you may know the speech or the play; don't concern yourself with that. Concern yourself rather with the words that you are facing on the printed page. For the purpose of the exercise it might even be more instructive if you have never seen the speech before. As I have said, eventually you will of course read the play and the scene and study the notes at the bottom of the page, which is part of your actor's homework. Your acting, though, can be energized and your imagination sparked when you do what Shakespeare's actors would have done—pick up the text, not unlike you would a side to do a cold reading, knowing that you had to go back into the audition room to perform it!

As you work on the speech you will continue to realize that Shakespeare has helped you. He has employed verbs, adjectives, similes, metaphors, and his own brand of onomatopoeia, which we spoke of in Lesson 3. Play these, each and every one, as you read; exaggerate and overdo them, making the verbs and the strange names larger and more elongated than even you might think necessary. Once again, assuming that you do not know the speech, what can you learn and discover from the words alone? Relying upon the lines before you, begin to write down what you have learned:

1. Who has Marcus encountered?
2. What is his relationship to her?
3. What has happened to her?
4. What are her injuries?
5. What does he feel?

See? You might not know it, but in doing this you have already started to act the speech. You don't need to rev yourself up to feel anything—yet. So you read on. You are faced with strange names and references: *Tereus, Titan, Philomela* (whom he calls "fair"), *Philomel, Cerberus,* and *Thracian.* Yes you will learn what these names and references refer to when you read the notes, but before then all you really need to know is that they are strange and foreign to you—uttered out of some descriptive need to *communicate the horror* of what has happened to Lavinia. You don't need to know specifically the meaning of these words yet; you just need to use them because you *have to speak,* in the same way you blurt out expletives or make up words *on the spot* when you can find no other words to express feelings that must be expressed!

You have been given enormously descriptive, helpful, onomatopoeic words to taste: *flies, lopp'd, hew'd, dream, wake* (these are examples, in the same sentence, of Shakespeare's other great indispensable tool, *antithesis*—more on that soon), *slumber, deflowered*. Do not—as I have seen beginning actors do—rush past these words; you will best tell your story by *over*-emphasizing them *because* you don't know what they mean! It might be that Marcus is so beside himself over Lavinia's rape and mutilation that he doesn't even know what he is saying, which will understandably overcome a person feeling emotion at the sight of a situation that is fantastically unexpected and out of the ordinary, made more so because of their love.

To practice this, perform the speech using all the values above, over and over again, as if you were trying to memorize it—which, in Shakespeare's day, you would have been trying to do—and take note of what this *action* does to you. You can apply the process to any of Shakespeare's long, famous emotional speeches, and not only those that are sad; you can do this to work on Benedick's "The world must be peopled!" speech from *Much Ado About Nothing*, Malvolio's "Do you come near me now!" from *Twelfth Night*, even Oberon's "I know a bank," and Titania's changeling child monologue from *A Midsummer Night's Dream*—in fact, any long speech the character is *forced* to speak out of need to express the desire of their heart.

Once more, at this point do not worry about feeling as much as about fighting as hard as you can to tell the *story* of the speech. This will help you begin to feel, but, more importantly, it will compel you to *do*.

I've thought of this little epigram that might help you remember this:

To portray feeling, think *in*-motion, not *e*-motion.

Exercise 16: My Cat is Dead

This continues the work from the Marcus speech. The title of it may sound frivolous, but the theme is the same. Continue to sense the arc and the *build* of emotion in a Shakespearean speech by adding layer upon layer of thoughts, just like the laying on of bricks, to build your "house" of personal tragic outcry. In my clumsy perhaps too obvious way I have listed below a growing font size in ascending order, to suggest the ever progressing feeling. But hold on: this is not to make you *try* to feel, or to arbitrarily get louder—no! The larger and larger sizes of the sentences are about the speaker fighting ever more *upward* to reach the *best* words to describe their horror.

Try this proclaiming out loud, "My cat is dead!" Then, fight to describe *everything* you can think of about

1. how your cat died
2. what your cat meant to you
3. the cruelty of the world to take your cat from you.

It might go like this:

> My cat is dead!
> Fluffy was my love, my cuddling buddy, my soft comfort!
> My joy in the night when I could not sleep!
> My warmth coming home after work!
> My laughter at watching her lick herself!
> Feeling her curl around me feet!
> She was so soft, so round, so furry!
> So playful, so skipping, so mouse-chasing!
> Her eyes so big, her paws so sharp,
> Her tail so furling,
> O world! O world! O world!
> O Fluffy, Fluffy, Fluffy!
> How shall I sleep?
> How shall I cuddle on the couch?

How shall I come home
    without her?
How, how, how . . . ?
MY CAT IS DEAD!

The speech could go on and on. It's a little silly of course, and I'm not the Bard of Avon. But you get the idea. Just remember such build also applies to the release of outrageous personal *joy*. The monologue might as well be titled, "My ice cream cone is great!" or "Sunday brunch is fantastic!" You don't need to use these phrases; I offer them simply to help guide you to a simple short sentence of your own choosing, that means something to *you*, which you can build upon as Shakespeare's characters in the throes of emotion build thought upon thought. Whatever phrase works for you. Perhaps you own a cat, or a dog, that you love as part of your family. Imagine what might happen to you if charged with describing, in as great detail as you can muster, the death of your beloved pet? Having just said that, I wonder if a few of you animal lovers might be getting a little misty-eyed right now. Have I struck a chord?

Shakespeare helps his actors build emotion not through the feeling first but rather out of the tremendous (outrageous) *need to communicate in words the depth of grief that tragedy has caused.* Marcus does this in *Titus*. As I said before, his speech must be long because the depth of his feeling is deep. Feeling first is not the idea, it is the active *doing* to *describe* feeling, which, yes, can lead to the performer *actually* feeling it *as* they are doing it. Get it?

But don't let me get knee-deep in dizzy acting-theory talk.

You can think of it as the simple brass tacks of laboring as a performer to get a show onto its feet *for this afternoon*. It's the same as what's on your mind when you re-enter that audition room to do that cold read after you have had a few minutes to look over the script. These long emotional speeches were probably handed to actors, not unlike Peter Quince passed them out to his fellow mechanicals in *Dream*, mere days if not hours before the show was to go on. There was *no* time to think about motivation! So the motivation had to be written into the words to help the actors "con them by rote" and *do it*!

What better way to coach actors as they work on a role?

Consider this long, famous, final speech of Katherina from *The Taming of the Shrew*. Admittedly there are complex issues associated with it because of how we think of a woman's role in society today versus how it was thought of in Shakespeare's time. But instead of getting bogged down with that, how about allowing the *audience* to address such issues in their own mind? This will rightly free you to do what you are there to do: get that show on its feet.

So as far as playing the scene, suppose you think of the speech in this way: as a simple proclamation of *love*?

> Fie, fie! Unknit that threatening unkind brow,
> And dart not scornful glances from those eyes,
> To wound thy lord, thy king, thy governor.
> It blots thy beauty as frosts do bite the meads,
> Confounds thy fame as whirlwinds shake fair buds,
> And in no sense is meet or amiable.
> A woman mov'd is like a fountain troubled,
> Muddy, ill-seeming, thick, bereft of beauty,
> And while it is so, none so dry or thirsty
> Will deign to sip or touch one drop of it.
> Thy husband is thy lord, thy life, thy keeper,
> Thy head, thy sovereign; one that cares for thee,
> And for thy maintenance; commits his body
> To painful labour both by sea and land,
> To watch the night in storms, the day in cold,
> Whilst thou liest warm at home, secure and safe;
> And craves no other tribute at thy hands
> But love, fair looks, and true obedience;

Too little payment for so great a debt.
Such duty as the subject owes the prince
Even such a woman oweth to her husband.
And when she is froward, peevish, sullen, sour,
And not obedient to his honest will,
What is she but a foul contending rebel
And graceless traitor to her loving lord?
I am asham'd that women are so simple
To offer war where they should kneel for peace,
Or seek for rule, supremacy, and sway,
When they are bound to serve, love, and obey.
Why are our bodies soft, and weak, and smooth,
Unapt to toil and trouble in the world,
But that our soft conditions and our hearts
Should well agree with our external parts?
Come, come, you froward and unable worms,
My mind hath been as big as one of yours,
My heart as great, my reason haply more,
To bandy word for word and frown for frown.
But now I see our lances are but straws,
Our strength as weak, our weakness past compare,
That seeming to be most which we indeed least are.
Then vail your stomachs, for it is no boot,
And place your hands below your husband's foot.
In token of which duty, if he please,
My hand is ready, may it do him ease.

In this way emotion (feeling) comes out of *doing*. This is the best way to approach the playing of emotion.

Exercise 17: The Last Line Six Times

Sometimes actors performing Shakespeare miss what is going on in the speech or scene by working too hard trying to "make sense" of the language. Sense is of course vital but we keep saying that it is already there waiting for the performer to play it in the words. This is why so often directors admonish their performers to just "say" it. Remember the Chorus in *Romeo and Juliet* talking about the "two hours' traffic of our stage"? As hard as it might sound, apparently the play's original run-time was something like two hours. *Two hours.* If this is possible the actors are going to need to build—and *keep up*—the near-locomotive energy of driving the play straight through to the end.

This lesson is to help you work on that drive, almost like a freight train, toward the *end* of a speech, which is often where you will find the reason why the person is moved to say it. It continues the discovery from the Marcus speech; it is not crazy to suggest that, done properly, the speaker might almost feel *tired* by the time they have finished, which helps plant the seeds of playing emotion. *In*-motion.

Try this example of Camillo, from *The Winter's Tale* (Act I, Scene 2). Say the *last* line of the monologue *six times*: once at the beginning of the speech, twice in the middle of the speech, and finally three times where it comes at the end (**bold** is my own).

Here comes Bohemia!
O miserable lady! But, for me,
What case stand I in? I must be the poisoner
Of good Polixenes; and my ground to do't
Is the obedience to a master, one
Who in rebellion with himself will have
All that are his so too.
Here comes Bohemia!
To do this deed,
Promotion follows. If I could find example
Of thousands that had struck anointed kings
And flourish'd after, I'ld not do't; but since
Nor brass nor stone nor parchment bears not one,
Let villany itself forswear't. **Here comes Bomehia!**
I must
Forsake the court: to do't, or no, is certain

To me a break-neck. Happy star, reign now!
Here comes Bohemia.
Here comes Bohemia.
Here comes Bohemia.

Then, *quickly*, start the speech again, without the repeating! Take note of what happens to you and to the driving momentum and need in the heart of Camillo.

Exercise 18: Grow from the Ground Up

This one may also work best committed to memory, but don't let that stop you. If it helps to start with just a few lines, do that. You can even do it just using one word at a time. The point is to choose enough lines so that you will be able to "grow"—that is, *build*.

Lie flat on the floor. Curl up into a ball.

- In a *low voice* start the speech.
- Continue to speak, with each line "growing."
- Grow to a spread-eagle on the floor, with your hands reaching outward.
- Grow to sitting position.
- Grow to crouching position.
- Grow to hands and knees.
- Grow to standing—all the while allow your hands to continue to reach upward.
- Grow higher and higher with your hands reaching toward the sky.
- Spring to the topmost point—at the end of the speech. Your hands are reaching up to the ceiling and your eyes are skyward.
- Your voice is at its *highest point* here!
- Now quickly do the speech again, standing, without the movement. Then check yourself and do it again. And again.

Exercise 19: Roll on the Floor

Yes I said it. Roll on the floor. Out of grief or joy it is within the realm of human possibility that people can be so moved—when faced with an outrageous situation caused by love— to fall down onto the floor and roll from side to side to show that emotion.

As you start the monologue, drop down onto the floor, and:

- Roll, from one side of the room to the other, as best you can.
- Speak the speech as you do this.
- Allow everything to happen; if your voice is affected, either loud or soft or closed off, *let it happen.*
- If you grow tired, *let it happen.*
- As you get dirty on the floor, *let it happen.*
- When you have completed the speech, clamor up to your feet as quickly as possible, and perform the monologue again!
- Take note of what, if anything, this does to the speech, and *you.*
- And do it again.

Now your question is probably *why*. Let me get personal for a moment and offer you this image from my own life, something I have witnessed. As a child, in the sad occasion when I have had to go to and witness a funeral—whether personal family member or not—I have seen people so overcome with grief that they physically collapsed—no, they did not pass out. I suspect that might have happened earlier, in private, when they first learned of their loved one's death. I am speaking about the body of the grieved being compelled to *give way* and *give out*, so that they literally had to be supported by well-wishers nearby. In the African American Baptist church tradition I grew up in I can remember middle-aged matrons dressed in white—you folks of a certain age know what I'm talking about—who are stationed in the church pews to be on the ready lest one of the parishioners get overcome with grief, either when the pastor strikes a certain tone in the middle of his sermon or during a certain song sung by the choir that causes them to remember a loved one who had passed on. These lovely matrons were always in white, with white gloves, stockings, and shoes even, and they were stationed at the ready to rush to the person overcome to try to console them, comfort them, physically support them, and even remove their spectacles so that they might not get broken if the person began to thrash about. This was a moment when the one overcome truly might fall down or even in some cases attempt to throw their own body onto the closed casket. And this was not only at funerals. It could occur at regular Sunday service, long after their beloved was gone, when a certain lyric from a hymn might cause them to remember their departed family member and they would, as we used to say, "Get happy." I once saw one lady simply rise up out of her seat and march up and down the aisle, in time, swinging her arms in time to the music, prancing, dancing, overcome with the near-hypnotic and almost ebullient trance that was a mixture of joy, sorrow, grief, remembrance, loss, and much more.

My friends, I suggest that if you let them, Shakespeare's *words* will compel you to do the same thing I saw these fine folks do so many years ago. And I'm not kidding. But don't forget: just like Exercises 1 and 2 these physical expressions come out of *happy celebration* as well as grief.

Have you ever been so happy that you nearly fell down, or just *had* to dance?

Exercise 20: Dueling Shakespeare

This improv requires two actors and is good for the classroom. Teachers, you can even choose the scenes ahead of time and assign them to the class, pairing up partners, and allow the actors to go over their lines ahead of time. But this is not crucial; as always great fun can happen even if nobody knows the lines at first.

Choose a very short scene from any Shakespeare play. It is best to pick scenes with one-line dialogue between characters; these will be easiest for the actors to pick up on the fly. The scenes should not be long, just three or four lines each, and the actors can always go back to the very beginning and start over. The idea is to get you into the habit of making big, theatrical choices, as many as you can think of, to act the scene.

It works this way: using these lines the two actors must "duel" one another, not unlike Wyatt Earp and Doc Holliday versus the Clanton Gang at the OK Corral, except instead of guns they must use the *lines* in the scene! Each actor will stalk, challenge, attack, shoot from the hip, firing off a round or a warning shot, etc., with *dialogue*. Then, the person "fired" at must respond in kind with their own Shakespeare line, back and forth, and so on.

The type of scene you choose might be this one from *Romeo and Juliet* (Act I, Scene 1):

SAMPSON
   Gregory, o' my word, we'll not carry coals.

GREGORY
   No, for then we should be colliers.

SAMPSON
   I mean, an we be in choler, we'll draw.

GREGORY
   Ay, while you live, draw your neck out o' the collar.

SAMPSON
   I strike quickly, being moved.

GREGORY
   But thou art not quickly moved to strike.

SAMPSON
   A dog of the house of Montague moves me.

Or instead of this opening scene with Gregory and Sampson you might pick the later scene and add Abraham so that the improv can become a brawl:

ABRAHAM
> Do you bite your thumb at us, sir?

SAMPSON
> I do bite my thumb, sir.

ABRAHAM
> Do you bite your thumb at us, sir?

SAMPSON
> [Aside to GREGORY] Is the law of our side, if I say ay?

GREGORY
> No.

SAMPSON
> No, sir, I do not bite my thumb at you, sir, but I bite my thumb, sir.

GREGORY
> Do you quarrel, sir?

ABRAHAM
> Quarrel sir! no, sir.

SAMPSON
> If you do, sir, I am for you: I serve as good a man as you.

ABRAHAM
> No better.

SAMPSON
> Well, sir.

GREGORY
> Say "better": here comes one of my master's kinsmen.

SAMPSON
> Yes, better, sir.

ABRAHAM
　You lie.

SAMPSON
　Draw, if you be men. Gregory, remember thy swashing
　　blow.

　And off they go. The aim is to *top* and *defeat* the opponent by the way you *perform your lines*. In playing the scene use the class as the audience, each actor playing directly to them as well as to each other to win the duel by getting students to be on their side. You can also do a variation on the exercise using longer scenes by giving them to the actors ahead of time, such as this marvelous sparring (a.k.a. wooing) moment from Act I Scene 1 of *Much Ado About Nothing*, between eventual lovers Beatrice and Benedick:

BEATRICE
　I wonder that you will still be talking, Signior Benedick:
　nobody marks you.

BENEDICK
　What, my dear Lady Disdain! are you yet living?

BEATRICE
　Is it possible disdain should die while she hath such meet
　food to feed it as Signior Benedick?
　Courtesy itself must convert to disdain, if you come in her
　presence.

BENEDICK
　Then is courtesy a turncoat. But it is certain I am loved of
　all ladies, only you excepted: and I
　would I could find in my heart that I had not a hard
　heart; for, truly, I love none.

BEATRICE
　A dear happiness to women: they would else have been
　troubled with a pernicious suitor. I thank God and my

cold blood, I am of your humour for that: I had rather
hear my dog bark at a crow than a man swear he
loves me.

BENEDICK

God keep your ladyship still in that mind! so some
gentleman or other shall 'scape a predestinate scratched
face.

BEATRICE

Scratching could not make it worse, an 'twere such a face
as yours were.

BENEDICK

Well, you are a rare parrot-teacher.

BEATRICE

A bird of my tongue is better than a beast of yours.

BENEDICK

I would my horse had the speed of your tongue, and so
good a continuer. But keep your way, i' God's name;
I have done.

BEATRICE

You always end with a jade's trick: I know you of old.

How do the dueling actors "win" the duel? How do they vanquish their foe? One way will be by getting the audience to *applaud*! That's right. Teacher, tell your students that this is the aim of their duel. Don't be shy or worry about being guilty of selfish claptrap; that is the point of this exercise! (However, be sure to remind them afterwards that the actor's aim is not to intentionally seek applause; it is to play the play!)

You can also try to win both physically as well as vocally. Using your voice you might:

elongate and exaggerate the vowels
hammer and pound the consonants

vary pitch up or down
do whatever you can think of with your voice.

Using your body you might:

crawl on the floor
bounce off the walls
shake like a leaf
dance a jig
whatever you can think of with your body.

This improvisation too is similar to "*Become* the Words." Acting Shakespeare is outrageous because for the "two hours' traffic" of a stage the performer must tell a story with those wonderful, never-before-heard words. Those words will require great use of your voice, of course, but you will need the full measure of your body and imagination as well to do it. Try the exercise with other "dueling" scenes from Shakespeare, such as between Oberon and Titania, Hermia and Helena, Demetrius and Lysander, and Theseus and Hippolyta in *A Midsummer Night's Dream*, or Petruchio and Katherina in *The Taming of the Shrew*. Find more on your own and try them!

Summary

Plays are about emotion, and it is the actor's job to portray this emotion. Doing this begins not out of attempting to *show* emotion; such a take is always unreliable as well as unbelievable. The best way—and rooted in the teaching of Stanislavsky, too—is in the performing of *physical actions*, which can be done over and over again because they are not bound by what the actor might actually feel in the moment. With these improvisations, the emotion comes out of *doing* something to *get* something. William Shakespeare helps you do this with his words. The best way to begin is by actually getting up on your feet, even when you might not know exactly what you are saying. That will come later. In performing these off-the-wall and sometimes crazy physical actions—with as much imagination and reckless abandon as your artistic soul can gather—you will be well on your way to "doing Shakespeare" as his actors might have done it at the moment they had been handed their scrolls.

Remember, think *in*-emotion, rather than *e*-motion.

Act Three

WORDS, WORDS, WORDS!

QUINCE
> Well, we will have such a prologue; and it shall be written in eight and six.

BOTTOM
> No, make it two more; let it be written in eight and eight.
>
> (*A Midsummer Night's Dream*)

How long a time lies in one little word!

(*Richard II*)

Now then: you have studied what little we know of Shakespeare's life and times and how theatre was done in Elizabethan England. You have gone over your monologue or scene with exercises and improvisations to find the "outrageous" in them. At this point you might wonder why it took so long to address more directly the one thing that sets William Shakespeare's plays far above dramatic literature in the history of the world: his poetry. The reason for this is very simple: *I want you to speak his words out loud before you do anything else.*

It might be blasphemous to say it but when you're just getting started I don't think you need to study Shakespeare's poetry. I think you need to *memorize* it and *do* it, and when you come to words or references you don't understand I ask that you fight through those, too, by using the *rest of the speech* to tell you what you have to do. If you do this you will have gotten closer than you realize to performing Shakespeare, and performing him faithfully. You can always add the richness and context that will come by taking a closer look at his words later; he constructed them not only so that his actors could learn their lines faster, he was actually directing them by showing them when to come in on cue, when to go fast or slow down, and even how to play moments for dramatic and comedic effect.

But if you would, dear friends, please bear this in mind: though we now take a peek at his poetic structure, I ask that you not lose the energy and fearlessness of the improvisational; these plays are, after all, written in *English*. In getting this far you have actually already "done" Shakespeare; this extra is gravy to help you "taste" him better. It is possible, if you allow it, for the analysis of iambic pentameter—as well as trochees, spondees, anapest, etc.—to blur your eyes just as dizzyingly as trigonometry. It's important to remember that the genesis of all Shakespeare's plays began as a story told to people gathered in a room (almost like it would be if you were performing a cold-read audition), and the audience won't be grading you on how scholarly your command of the language is; we want to know if, along the way, you were able to move us so much that we leave the theater sighing, "Boy. That *is* like life, isn't it?"

Thou and *You*

In your study of Shakespearean text, you will be introduced to his constant artful use of the formal address of *thou* and *you*. Their usage goes back to Old and Middle English and was further influenced by the French with the Norman Conquests of 1066, but you, who are an actor and not a linguist, can simply concentrate on the fact that these words of greeting are not necessarily present out of some archaic classical tradition alone.

They possess a down-to-earth character agenda, placed there as much to portray attitude and emotional relationship as to hold to social ceremony. Additional iterations of *thou* and *you* include *thee, thine, thy, thyself, your, yours,* and *yourself/selves*.

Below is a listing of when and how you might see them used in Shakespeare:

You
When upper class are talking to each other
A character talks to someone far from them on the stage

Thou
Lower class to each other
Masters to servants
Parents to children
Superiors to inferiors   (I suggest *your* can do the same thing)
Talking to a lover
Talking to God or a god
Talking to a character who is absent
Talking to a character near you on the stage

Thou and *you* and their various forms appear in all of Shakespeare's plays and poems. I have chosen *As You Like It* to demonstrate what the Bard might be up to.

Let's look at *you* and *your*. In Act I, Scene 1, the evil Oliver addresses his younger brother Orlando, whom he has subjugated in poverty. They are of the same social status, being sons of a wealthy landowner. The actors playing these roles can know that the words are an argument; what can also be deduced in the use of *you* is Oliver and Orlando's attitude toward each other—one keeping the other down, the other finally having gotten to the point where he will not take it anymore. **Bold** is my own:

OLIVER

Now, sir! what make **you** here?

ORLANDO

Nothing: I am not taught to make any thing.

OLIVER

What mar **you** then, sir?

ORLANDO

Marry, sir, I am helping **you** to mar that which God made, a poor unworthy brother of **yours**, with idleness.

OLIVER

Marry, sir, be better employed, and be naught awhile.

ORLANDO

Shall I keep **your** hogs and eat husks with them? What prodigal portion have I spent, that I should come to such penury?

OLIVER

Know **you** where **you** are, sir?

ORLANDO

O, sir, very well; here in **your** orchard.

OLIVER

Know **you** before whom, sir?

ORLANDO

Ay, better than him I am before knows me. I know **you** are my eldest brother; and, in the gentle condition of blood, **you** should so know me. The courtesy of nations allows **you** my better, in that **you** are the first-born; but the same tradition takes not away my blood, were there twenty brothers betwixt us: I have as much of my father in me as **you**; albeit, I confess, **your** coming before me is nearer to his reverence.

OLIVER

What, boy!

ORLANDO
  Come, come, elder brother, **you** are too young in this.

OLIVER
  Wilt **thou** lay hands on me, villain?

You and *your* can also be spoken out of a desire to rebuff, ridicule, or chastise. Rosalind does this to Phebe in Act III, Scene 5, when she uses *you* and *your* 25 times in the speech! (The full speech is available to you in the "Practice Speeches" appendix.)

Also notice that the last line of Oliver above includes the address *thou*. *Thou* is often used when people of the upper class are addressing the lower class, or those beneath them in some way, such as masters to servants or parents to children. Oliver is not speaking to a child or an actual servant, but he is displaying his disdainful attitude toward his younger brother, considering Orlando *beneath him*, which I say is also displayed in his use of *you* and *your*. Acting verbs such as to "put down" or our contemporary "diss" (as in *dis*respect) comes to mind. Also, when characters change from *thou* to *you* or *you* to *thou* this too can indicate a change in the relationship, which in this case is exactly what is happening. You can say that, though the two brothers have been involved in strife for years, this scene represents a "falling out," in which Oliver has also had enough. In the scene that follows he calls his servant Charles the wrestler to get him to murder Orlando in a wrestling match.

Another example of the use of *thou*, *thy*, and *thine* comes later, when the put-upon Oliver is given his come-uppance by Duke Frederick, as the Duke threatens him in Act III, Scene 1. I continue to use **bold**:

DUKE FREDERICK
  Not see him since? Sir, sir, that cannot be:
  But were I not the better part made mercy,
  I should not seek an absent argument
  Of my revenge, **thou** present. But look to it:

Find out **thy** brother, wheresoe'er he is;
Seek him with candle; bring him dead or living
Within this twelvemonth, or turn **thou** no more
To seek a living in our territory.
Thy lands and all things that **thou** dost call **thine**
Worth seizure do we seize into our hands,
Till **thou** canst quit **thee** by **thy** brothers mouth
Of what we think against **thee**.

OLIVER
O that your highness knew my heart in this!
I never loved my brother in my life.

DUKE FREDERICK
More villain **thou**. Well, push him out of doors;
And let my officers of such a nature
Make an extent upon his house and lands:
Do this expediently and turn him going.

In a kindlier way Orlando speaks to his longtime elderly servant Adam in Act II, Scene 3:

O good old man, how well in **thee** appears
The constant service of the antique world,
When service sweat for duty, not for meed!
Thou art not for the fashion of these times,
Where none will sweat but for promotion,
And having that, do choke their service up
Even with the having: it is not so with **thee**.
But, poor old man, **thou** prunest a rotten tree,
That cannot so much as a blossom yield
In lieu of all thy pains and husbandry.
But come **thy** ways; we'll go along together,
And ere we have **thy** youthful wages spent,
We'll light upon some settled low content.

You also find *thou* in private sacred moments, such as in prayer or a plea to the gods or God, and in moments between close devoted friends. Below begins Act I, Scene 2 between Celia and Rosalind. The two maidens go back and forth between *thou* and *thee*. This shift can also suggest a change in the relationship during the scene (this change might perhaps be what actors of today might call "beats"); Celia is concerned that her life-long childhood friend is down in the dumps over her precarious position at court with Duke Frederick, Celia's father:

CELIA
>Herein I see **thou** lov'st me not with the full weight that I love **thee**. If my uncle, **thy** banished father, had banished **thy** uncle, the Duke my father, so **thou** hadst been still with me, I could have taught my love to take **thy** father for mine. So wouldst **thou**, if the truth of **thy** love to me were so righteously tempered as mine is to **thee**.

ROSALIND
>Well, I will forget the condition of my estate to rejoice in **yours**.

CELIA
>**You** know my father hath no child but I, nor none is like to have; and truly, when he dies, **thou** shalt be his heir, for what he hath taken away from **thy** father perforce, I will render **thee** again in affection. By mine honor I will, and when I break that oath, let me turn monster. Therefore, my sweet Rose, my dear Rose, be merry.

ROSALIND
>From henceforth I will, coz, and devise sports. Let me see—what think **you** of falling in love?

CELIA
>Marry, I prithee do, to make sport withal; but love no man in good earnest, nor no further in sport neither than with safety of a pure blush **thou** mayst in honor come off again.

Act III, Scene 5 has a private little moment between Silvius and Phebe. It can be considered a scene between lovers, though at this point in the play Phebe is actually in love with Ganymede (Rosalind in disguise) and Silvius is drunk with love for Phebe:

PHEBE
>Ha, what sayst **thou**, Silvius?

SILVIUS
>Sweet Phebe, pity me.

PHEBE
>Why, I am sorry for **thee**, gentle Silvius.

SILVIUS
>Wherever sorrow is, relief would be.
>If you do sorrow at my grief in love,
>By giving love your sorrow and my grief
>Were both extermined.

PHEBE
>**Thou** hast my love. Is not that neighbourly?

SILVIUS
>I would have you.

PHEBE
>Why, that were covetousness.
>Silvius, the time was that I hated **thee**;
>And yet it is not that I bear **thee** love;
>But since that **thou** canst talk of love so well,
>**Thy** company, which erst was irksome to me,
>I will endure, and I'll employ **thee** too.
>But do not look for further recompense
>Than **thine** own gladness that **thou** art employed . . .
>Know'st **thou** the youth that spoke to me erewhile?

Phebe has just fallen in love with Ganymede and is quietly pondering that love. She uses Silvius's love for her as a means to get him to deliver a letter to Ganymede. It might even be a valid acting choice that Phebe *woos* Silvius to accomplish this.

Other iterations of *thou* include addressing someone who is not in the scene with you or who is otherwise near to you on the stage, and *you* when one character is speaking to someone far from them on the stage, such as Malcolm in the final scene in *Macbeth* as he speaks to his victorious countrymen spread about the stage:

> We shall not spend a large expense of time
> Before we reckon with **your** several loves,
> And make us even with **you**.

So let me say once more—because by now you know that I can't resist the opportunity to repeat myself—that in Shakespeare's language and in fact all language placed in the mouths of characters by a playwright, even the most reverent ceremonial-*seeming* words of address are spoken not always out of mere courtesy alone, and even Shakespeare himself from time to time will appear to break his own "rules" for his own dramatic purpose. Especially when a character changes midstream from *thou* to *you* or vice versa; you can trust that this means something that will be very useful to you. What you want to do is look at these instances as driven by *circumstance* and *context*, depending upon the *human need* in the heart of the speaker.

The Poetry That Doesn't Rhyme

But in spite of what we just talked about, contrary to popular belief Elizabethans did not necessarily walk around speaking *thee* and *thou* to each other. Shakespeare chose the language of his plays first to heighten the experience of theatre for his audience, and second to differentiate his characters from each other, such as the upper class from the lower class. However, it is not as simple as saying, "The lower-class characters always speak in prose and the rich and high-born always speak in verse." This is only partly true; it is more accurate and helpful to say that in a given scene characters speak the language *which best fits their need.* Henry V moves back and forth between poetry and prose, one moment wreaking havoc in blank verse with his grand, Saint Crispin's Day speech and the next moment commiserating his lowly beaten-down soldiers around the campfire in everyday prose. Iago speaks both poetry and prose with Rodrigo and then poetry with Othello. Rosalind certainly speaks verse in the court but then prose in the Forest of Arden (where, to escape death from her cruel uncle, she has also disguised herself as a boy). *The Merry Wives of Windsor*, a play about simple country ladies playing tricks on Sir John Falstaff, is written almost entirely in prose. Look to the situation of the play these characters are dealing with as well as their station in life to find out why they suddenly change back and forth: you might soon realize that they are serving their *own ends*, and their predicament makes it necessary to move nimbly in their speech, back and forth as the situation demands. For instance, studying Iago's words in *Othello* might suggest to you that the famous villain is using plain-speaking prose as he conspires with Rodrigo, but then he turns to blank verse for flowery images to convince the doomed young man he still has a chance with Desdemona. With Othello he speaks verse out of (at least feigned) respect from soldier to superior, but also the heightened language is meant to convince the Moor of Desdemona's unfaithfulness in the same way he duped Rodrigo. In *As You Like It* Rosalind, well-bred and high-born, is capable of speaking verse at court out of respect for both the bad Duke Frederick and love for her friend Celia; then, once disguised as a boy in Arden, she speaks prose—not out of evil but rather out of a desire to convincingly playing her role, speaking the tongue of the local natives to help them believe she is actually a male from those parts. In the same play Silvius, though of the country, speaks verse as he pleads his love for Phebe; Phebe does the same—as she lovingly praises Ganymede (Rosalind in boy's garb). *Merry Wives* takes place in a country setting with normal, home-spun folks; Falstaff is speaking the prose of the "lower" class because his *intentions*—fornication with married ladies—are *low*. But when pure young lovers Fenton and Anne Page converse in private, they speak blank verse. These are just a few of the possibilities—character, actor-driven possibilities, mind you—that can be unearthed when delving into the construction of Shakespeare's text to find out what his characters are going through. He has placed into the hands of his actors what their characters think and who they are in part by the *arrangement* of their words on the printed page.

Maybe you have been told by your acting teacher from time to time that you get too precious with the *pause*. Actors love to pause. Those brief moments give us exquisite space to demonstrate to the audience just how brilliant, how talented, how limitless is our depth of feeling as a performer. If you are like me you might have been guilty of doing what every actor just starting out seems to do: you pause *before* you reply, no doubt in an attempt to give yourself time within those milliseconds to *feel* it before you answer the cue line. Maybe—and please don't think that I am jumping on you, because I have done the same thing myself—in the very back of your mind you do this not only so that you can feel it, but in order that the *audience* can *see* you feel it, as well! Deadly! Your director will hasten to admonish you never to do this, of course. They will rightly say that the time spent by the audience waiting for your reply will only slow down the play, so they instruct you to do all of your reacting *as* you are speaking. Throughout your career you will no doubt hear this age-old acting tip again and again, even if spoken to others: act *on* the line.

Shakespeare probably never said it that way but he would have been right in league with your director. More than likely English actors spoke far more rapidly than we do today. Although your normal inclination in studying the poetic meter of Shakespeare's speeches is to try to find clues on what might be working in the mind of a character in a certain moment—and that is the best reason for studying his verse—when you break down the poetry it can also help you with one of the actor's most pressing obligations—*picking up your cues.* In speaking blank verse—that is, a stanza of poetry that does not rhyme—you will best make sense of it if you adhere to a very simple principle—*follow the punctuation.* Even if in the throes of "feeling it," an actor still needs to be careful of and to avoid pausing—stopping, breaking—in the middle of a line that is not otherwise broken by a period, comma, colon, semi-colon, or *caesura.* You are not playing Stanley Kowalski. (In case you don't know Tennessee Williams's famous character from *A Streetcar Named Desire,* I should mention that in theatrical lore he has forever been linked with an actor's predilection for mumbling realism on the stage.) Unnecessarily breaking up text makes it harder to make sense of the line you are speaking. This is true even in contemporary plays. In keeping strict adherence to the punctuation you will make the most amazing of all Shakespearean discoveries; this is what directors and acting teachers—and perhaps even the prompters in Shakespeare's time—mean when they exclaim, "Just *say* it!"

Now I am not saying that the actor, even when speaking Shakespearean verse, can *never* pause, even in the middle of a line. We are not setting down hard and fast rules here. What I am saying is that before you rightly make the acting choice that will help to bring your character to life, it is most helpful to begin with the fundamental meaning of the line—and that will always begin with the punctuation the writer intended in the first place (in the Bard's case this means what we have best been able to put together after 400 years). Just as you master arithmetic before you tackle algebra, try first to discover the *best* meaning of a playwright's line, and then the vocal heights to which you soar are rightfully up to you. (This by the way is true of contemporary plays, as well.) You can then pause when the urge strikes you—as long as you don't *slow down the show*!

The technical term for this form of Shakespearean poetry I have just described is iambic pentameter. This is the form of language you will most often see when working on Shakespeare.

But don't let such a mathematical-sounding phrase daunt you; actually iambic pentameter is very simple in its meaning. Meter is the way poetic verse is constructed to be better understood. This meter is broken down into various forms, depending upon the desire of the poet, and in this case it is a pattern of consistently recurring *unstressed and stressed syllables.* When you highlight the unstressed and stressed syllable into a single component this is called a "foot." This single foot is also called an *iamb,* a "foot" of poetic meter composed of two syllables, one unstressed and one stressed. Such as, "To *be.*" Next add the word *penta.* Penta means "five." Add *meter* to the end of that and when you put these together you get *iambic pentameter,* or a foot of unstressed/stressed syllables that happens five times in a line of blank verse poetry, which creates what is called a "regular" line that "scans" (calculates) into a ten-syllable line divided between five (iambic) feet. Are you dizzy yet? Don't be. The word *scansion* is another fancy word for studying the breakdown of poetic verse in just this way. The word scan comes from the Latin *scandere,* which loosely means "to ascend." This is actually quite instructive. In studying poetic meter you are, in effect, *ascending toward the meaning* of the line of poetry. I like thinking of it this way, because to me it suggests *action* and it suggests *movement, doing* something. As an actor you aren't studying the arrangement of iambs on a page for some great academic thesis; you're trying to find out what is driving a character's need to *speak.*

These are the basics of blank verse and it is in this form that you will find the majority of Elizabethan plays and sonnets, not just Shakespeare. This will be the principal form you should devote your initial study of his verse upon. There are many other forms of poetic meter which will really make your head spin, such as trochees—when the syllable is stressed, *then* unstressed; anapests—two soft stresses then hard stress; dactyls—one stressed then two unstressed; and amphibrach—unstressed, stressed, unstressed. But let's hold our horses and make sure we are clear on the most common Shakespearean verse you will most likely work with first!

So; on to doing. A "regular" line only means that the line of iambic pentameter seems to flow more or less easily and logically from your tongue *as long as you speak it aloud adhering to the punctuation*. (In addition to helping you make better sense of what you are saying, this recognition makes it clear just how much faster and fleet of tongue Elizabethan actors were, much more so than some of our fellow mumbling, Method-influenced actors of today.) Eventually you will be able to tap out the rhythm of iambic pentameter the way you would slap your thigh with your hand or tap your toe to beat the rhythm of musical syncopation—poetry is music—and you will further find that this particular rhythm, this unstressed/stressed beat, tends to replicate the beat of the *pumping of the human heart*. See below the arrangement of two syllables, in five segments (feet). If you speak it out loud you might say it like this:

da *dum* / da *dum* / da *dum* / da *dum* / da *dum*.

There. You have just spoken a *regular* iambic line.

Is it possible, in looking at the example above as well as speaking it aloud (even though I have used italics to indicate the stressed syllable), that you get a sense of a heart beating? Thuh-*thump*, thuh-*thump*, thuh-*thump*, etc.?

Earlier I used the word "regular," in speaking about an iambic Shakespearean line. You might ask: what does this "regular" have to do with acting Shakespeare?

Again I repeat: when you have an unfettered line of iambic pentameter you can most likely speak the line easily, directly, and simply—as long as you don't stop in the middle of an uninterrupted line. If you are able to speak to your peers without intermittent stops and false starts you are clearer and you make better sense, and it might be deduced that the thoughts driving your words are reasonably clear to you. You might even believe that you are in either a *state of well-being* or that you at least possess *clarity* in what you are trying to say. In other words, you understand *what* you are saying and *why*, and this normal, human delivery of speech is most likely going to flow in a beat-of-the-human-heart rhythm as the words fall effortlessly from your lips.

Then the light bulb pops on.

A regular line of blank verse is probably spoken by a character who is in touch with what they want and are able to communicate it. They are probably not confused or distracted—though this does not mean that they are not in turmoil or otherwise unhappy; a regular iambic line is also spoken by a character in distress; it may simply be they are not so emotionally broken up about it that their words are broken up in the meter as well. Shakespeare uses regular lines when his characters are hysterical, as well. Once you have arrived at this you will have hit upon the best use of the technique of scansion!

In playing Shakespearean speeches you will still be able to just "get up and do it," but isn't it helpful to have this handy-dandy *tool* for you to resort to in the event that you might have questions about what a line seems to be saying, and therefore need a little more help? (Especially after you have already gone to the trouble of reading the text notes at the bottom of the page!)

Though there are other poetic techniques Shakespeare employs to break up a regular line when his characters are going through something that is making them hard to understand—such as *trochaic* pentameter—there is also a lunch-pail, working-actor reason for the meter that beats like the pumping of the human heart: number one, for the most part we human beings tend to speak this unstressed/stressed pattern of speech in our everyday lives, and two—for performers who have a job to do—such poetic rhythm can be memorized *quickly.* I have already said that as a member of the Lord Chamberlain's Men you might have been handed your part today for a performance this afternoon. In constructing his plays in this fashion Shakespeare, an actor himself, is giving his fellow tragedians a helping hand because he knew they had to pick up quickly on multiple parts and plays during the course of a week. Whew!

The Joys of Iambic Pentameter

There are many possibilities in Shakespeare's orchestration of blank verse. It can also indicate stage direction and action. You will find lines that may appear "*ir*regular" at first; that is, they do not follow the standard ten syllables spread over five feet of iambic pentameter. But when you look closer at the text—as long it has not been "corrected" by some editors; go for the Pelican or Folger if not the First Folio to be safe—you will see that it is still actually meant to be spoken as iambic pentameter because the words were intended to be *shared* with another character in the *next* speech!

Shared Lines

Not to make your head swirl again, but look at this example from *Macbeth* (Act II, Scene 2):

LADY MACBETH
   I heard the owl scream and the crickets cry.
   Did not you speak?

MACBETH
                      When?

LADY MACBETH
                            Now.

MACBETH
                                As I descended?

LADY MACBETH
   Ay.

MACBETH
                  Hark!—Who lies i' the second chamber?

LADY MACBETH
   Donalbain.

MACBETH
   This is a sorry sight.

LADY MACBETH
    A foolish thought, to say a sorry sight!

You can see the movement of the speeches on the printed page but even more effective is listening to actors picking up their cues very rapidly, nearly overlapping one another. Shakespeare having Macbeth and Lady Macbeth share this series of blank verse lines serves the mood and moment and it serves the actors on stage, too: the castle is cold and it is the middle of the night. Being urged on by his wife, Macbeth has just murdered King Duncan sleeping upstairs—the bloody knives are still in his bloody hands—and the two of them, husband and wife, are thrown into disastrous calamity. No pretty-sounding soliloquies are necessary here (they will be delivered later); all that is needed is human *panic*—the alert, alive, fearful words toppling over one another because these two people have no idea what they are going to do next. In distress don't people interrupt and talk over each other? Again, the choices made by the hand of Shakespeare—even if grammatically, thematically, rhetorically ground-breaking at the same time—first and foremost are there to serve the actor performing in the Globe at two o'clock that afternoon!

See here another example, this from *Hamlet* (Act I, Scene 1). As you know, "something is rotten in the state of Denmark." The good King Hamlet has died and his brother Claudius has taken his throne and married his widow Gertrude; it is in the small hours of the morning and soldiers are on the watch. They claim that the night before they saw the Ghost of the dead king walking about, and it has scared them out of their wits. (And by the way; would not *you* think it outrageous to see a ghost?) So Shakespeare has written it in such a way that to speak it as written is to *act* it; short, quick, harsh, nearly overlapped, because these men are confused and afraid:

FRANCISCO
    Give you good night.

MARCELLUS

                    O, farewell, honest soldier:
Who hath relieved you?

FRANCISCO

                    Barnardo has my place.
Give you good night.

Exit Francisco.

MARCELLUS

                    Holla! Barnardo!

BARNARDO

                              Say—
What, is Horatio there?

HORATIO

                    A piece of him.

In the beginning you might wonder "what's up with that?" when Shakespeare spreads his poetic lines over the course of two—or more—people speaking. Well, with both these examples you can believe that these are possibly *stage directions*, telling actors who only just now got their scrolls *how to play the scene.* Punctuation choice can also indicate overlapping to indicate nervous lovers completing each other's sentences, gulping over one another at first loving glance, or it can mean haste as people are driving toward feverish action in war or impending death. It can even indicate physical action, where Shakespeare might be providing space for the actor to perform stage business of some sort. This is called an imperfect line, and a very good example appears in Act IV, Scene 3, of *Romeo and Juliet,* when Juliet says:

    My dismal scene I needs must act alone.
    Come, vial.

You notice in studying that the first line—"My dismal scene . . ."—is actually a regular line followed by an irregular line which only has two words: "Come, vial." A blank space is left where the rest of the four feet should be. This is called a *spondee*, which is a foot of poetry consisting of two stressed syllables. Scholars—such as you are now—may rightly theorize that here Shakespeare is providing the actor with blocking for the scene, telling you that here is where the terrified, conflicted teenage Juliet rises out of bed to take up the vial from her nightstand—words put together by the world's greatest playwright not because of some pedagogical urge but because of theatrical, acting necessity. Don't you just know that this kind of writing must have also included long speeches placed in the right spot to give a previously exiting character sufficient time to make an otherwise too-quick costume change?

Shakespeare also provides these acting beats within Hamlet's "rogue and peasant slave" speech in Act II, Scene 2, such as:

For Hecuba!
O, vengeance!

And he closes the soliloquy with perhaps the most famous of all "capping" couplets (we'll touch on them shortly), foretelling of things to come:

> . . . I'll have grounds
> More relative than this: the play's the thing
> Wherein I'll catch the conscience of the king.

Poetic meter meant to *direct* you as well as move you.

A Feminine Ending

Sometimes an iambic line will not end with a clear stop. We will see this with the first line of a Claudius speech in a moment; an extra unstressed beat at the *end*. I know this is sexist, but scholars call this a *weak*, or *feminine*, ending. A good example of this is Hamlet's "To be or not to be" speech (my **bold** signifies stressed syllables, *italic* signifies unstressed syllable):

To **be**, / or **not** / to **be**: / that **is** / the **ques-** / *-tion*

To act feminine/weak endings I suggest thinking of them like this: imagine when you bend over and scramble for a loose scrap of paper that blows out of your hands in the wind, causing you to have to chase after it. You go through fits and starts of trying to snatch up the piece of paper, not quite able to retrieve it; it is an important piece of paper, a valuable document you must not allow to get out of your hands. Suppose you consider this when playing the end of the uncertain, "weak," last line: *you are struggling to find an answer that keeps getting away, and though you might first blurt an attempt at an answer you realize midstream that you actually don't have the answer and so you lose steam at the end of your sentence.* Your final words lose emphasis—because of being *unable to find an answer.*

However, as you do this just remember not to let this inability to find an answer cause you to drop volume/energy at the end of the line. Please take this rule: *struggling to find an answer should drive and energize you, not slow you down!*

More Tools from Shakespeare's Arsenal

Here are a few more of Shakespeare's verse tools:

Trochee—stressed then unstressed: *dum*-de, etc. Such as the spell cast by the Weird Sisters in *Macbeth*:

Dou-ble, / *Dou*-ble / *Toil* and / *Trou*-ble;
Fi-re / *Burn*, and / *Cal*-dron / *Bub*-ble

Does not the rhythm of this meter sound and suggest aggression? Building, advancing, pounding forward?

Anapest—unstressed/unstressed then stressed: de-de-*dum*

Alexandrine—a line of verse having six iambic feet; the English reference for hexameter

Dactyl—stressed then unstressed/unstressed: *dum*-de-de

Spondee—stressed/stressed: *dum-dum*

Pyrrhic—unstressed/unstressed: de-de

Tetrameter—four iambic feet

Hexameter—six iambic feet, most often dactylic and found in Greek and Latin grand poetry, such as Homer's *Iliad*

Elision—when an unstressed vowel, consonant, or syllable is dropped to make a line of verse scan to 10 or 11 syllables. Such as "i" for "in," "on't" for "on it" and "o'er" for "over."

Caesura—a pause, with or without punctuation, halfway through a verse line.

Scansion in Action

To get a sense of how you might use scansion here is a cutting from Claudius's long prayer in *Hamlet*, Act III, Scene 3 (the full speech is in the "Practice Speeches" appendix). For unstressed syllables you can see the ˇ symbol; the forward slash / is to indicate stressed syllables.

```
  ˇ    /  ˇ   /  ˇ   /  ˇ   /    ˇ     /
O, my/ offence /is rank /it smells/ to heaven;/
  ˇ    /   ˇ    /  ˇ  /  ˇ     /  ˇ    /
It hath/ the pri/mal el/dest curse up/on't,/
  ˇ      /  ˇ    /   ˇ
A broth/er's mur/der./ Pray can I not,/
    ˇ       /  ˇ  /  ˇ   /  ˇ     /   ˇ   /
Though in/clin a/tion be /as sharp /as will:
   ˇ      /   ˇ     /    ˇ    /   ˇ     / ˇ    /
My stron/ger guilt /defeats/ my strong/ intent;/
```

```
  ˘    /   ˘   /  ˘    /  ˘    /   ˘        /
And, like/ a man /to dou/ble bus/iness bound,/
  ˘   /  ˘   /      ˘     /   ˘    /   ˘  /
I stand/ in pause /where I/ shall first/ begin,/
  ˘   /   ˘   /   ˘   /   ˘    /   ˘      /
And both/ neglect./ What if/ this cur/sed hand/
   ˘    /  ˘    /  ˘  /  ˘   /  ˘     /
Were thick/er than/ itself / with broth/er's blood,
  ˘     /   ˘    /  ˘   /   ˘    /  ˘       /
Is there / not rain / enough / in the sweet heav/ ens
  ˘   /   ˘    /   ˘   /    ˘    /  ˘       /
To wash/ it white/ as snow?/ Whereto /serves mercy
  ˘   /   ˘    /   ˘    /  ˘   /  ˘    /
But to / confront / the vis /age of /offence?/
```

In this largely iambic monologue there are a few lines that do not scan into regular lines. In the very first line, "O, my offence is rank, it smells to *heav*-en," "heaven" is a word that is stressed on the first syllable, *heav*. It comes at the end of the sentence, so you see the instance of the *feminine ending*. It happens again at the end of the line, "Is there not rain enough in the sweet heavens." *Heav* is again stressed, making it necessary to soften *ens* in order to best preserve the regular line meter. Then there's the line "A brother's murder. Pray can I not." Here we have a troubled thought from Claudius times *two*, in the form of a spondee, two accented syllables in a line—*dum dum*—and in this case a *double* spondee: "Pray, can, I, not." This occurrence should set the alarm bells tingling; you can know that *something* is causing shifts and turns in Claudius's mind, all related to what he is praying for and why. Remember: in the *words themselves*, even before you begin rhythmic analysis, Shakespeare has Claudius *tell* the audience what he is going through; the viewing listener will learn that Claudius is feeling guilty over having murdered his own brother and he has finally been driven to prayer to God on high for some last gasp of solace, some hope for forgiveness. But, sadly for him, by the end of the speech Claudius realizes that he wasn't really willing to repent after all, his getting down on his knees was all for nothing. *The actor knows this just from picking up the text and reading it aloud,* but for extremely helpful extra study, the change in the verse can guide the actor to additional choices that will enrich performance through greater nuance.

This is the value of scansion. It is not meant to *demand* that you do one thing or another thing; it is merely available to you as a little bit of additional help in your scene analysis after you feel you already know what is going on in your character's mind. Look on what you discover—the breakup of the meter—as potential red flags, with the Bard alerting you, "Hey! Take another quick look at this moment, would you?"

Rhymed Verse and Couplets: A Poet and *Do* Know It

Shakespeare has his characters speak rhyme verse for several reasons. It can be for songs (such as those sung by Feste in *Twelfth Night*, or Ariel in *The Tempest*); for Choruses, Prologues and Epilogues (*Romeo and Juliet, Henry V, A Midsummer Night's Dream,* etc.); plays-within-plays (*Hamlet* and *Dream*); and to depict the supernatural fairy world (*Macbeth, Tempest,* and *Dream*). With rhyme, in addition to cap a scene or suggest that something is going to happen, I say that Shakespeare's characters are also *speaking out of their greatest need.* Below are examples of how he does this.

Richard II: Bolingbroke (the future King Henry IV) speaks rhyme only after he has attained the crown.

Twelfth Night: the grieving Olivia speaks in prose—until she becomes infatuated with Cesario (the woman-disguised-as-man Viola) and she suddenly turns to rhyme!

Romeo and Juliet: in Act III, Scene 1, in the aftermath of the confused brawl that led to Mercutio and Tybalt's death, Benvolio begins first with blank verse to confess how it happened and ends with a rhyme, followed by Lady Capulet's plea for Romeo's death. The Prince ends the scene with a long all-rhyming speech as he banishes Romeo from Verona.

Measure for Measure: in Act III, Scene 2, Duke Vincentio (disguised as a monk) encounters Elbow and Pompey and they play a scene totally in prose. When the others exit, the Duke speaks a long monologue entirely in rhyme, as he tells the audience of the perils of false faith, such as, in part:

> Shame to him whose cruel striking
> Kills for faults of his own liking!
> Twice treble shame on Angelo,
> To weed my vice and let his grow!
> O, what may man within him hide,
> Though angel on the outward side!

Rhymed couplets are two consecutive lines of verse that end with the last word in each line rhyming. The word couplet comes from the French *couple*, which means "a little pair." This is fitting.

In studying *Hamlet* you are introduced to this early, in Act I, Scene 2, when in describing his outward appearance the Prince of Denmark says (**bold** mine):

> But I have that within which passeth **show**;
> These but the trappings and the suits of **woe**.

At the end of that scene, shocked upon hearing Horatio's rumor of having seen the Ghost of Hamlet's father on the battlements, Hamlet ends his short speech with:

> Till then sit still, my soul: foul deeds will **rise**,
> Though all the earth o'erwhelm them, to men's **eyes**.

Couplets can even appear a line before the end of the speech, such as when Hamlet closes Act I, Scene 4 with:

> So, gentlemen,
> With all my love I do commend me to you:
> And what so poor a man as Hamlet is
> May do, to express his love and friending to you,
> God willing, shall not lack. Let us go in together;
> And still your fingers on your lips, I pray.
> The time is out of joint: O cursed **spite**,
> That ever I was born to set it **right**!
> Nay, come, let's go together.

Such couplets as these are called "capping" couplets, because they are meant to "cap" or end a scene with a particular force or flourish. This rhyming flourish is not to be taken as merely a witty turn of phrase—although you know that it can be at least that—it should be a foreshadowing, a warning if you will, of things to come, either of foreboding or of joy. Today we would call it an "exit line," and as with all exit lines it must be spoken so clearly that every single person in the audience will know beyond a shadow of a doubt that something *big* is coming! Below are a few more capping couplets that end a scene:

> O time! thou must untangle this, not I;
> It is too hard a knot for me to untie!
> 			(Viola, *Twelfth Night,* Act II, Scene 2)

> I'll tell him yet of Angelo's request,
> And fit his mind to death, for his soul's rest.
> 			(Isabella, *Measure for Measure,* Act II, Scene 4)

> A gentle riddance. Draw the curtains, go.
> Let all of his complexion choose me so.
> 			(Portia, *The Merchant of Venice,* Act II, Scene 7)

Also, when rhymed couplets appear in a scene between two characters, play them as if you are *picking up on and attempting to complete the other person's thought.* Below is an example of Hermia and Helena from *A Midsummer Night's Dream* (Act I, Scene 1). As the scene begins they are not actually sharing couplets but like the earlier example from *Macbeth* it does illustrate how characters in need of one another share lines back and forth, on top of each other's utterance, as they fight to help each other, and later Hermia does venture into rhyme to seek a greater proclamation of her love and devotion to Lysander.

HERMIA
My good Lysander!
I swear to thee, by Cupid's strongest bow,
By his best arrow with the golden head,
By the simplicity of Venus' doves,
By that which knitteth souls and prospers loves,
And by that fire which burn'd the Carthage queen,
When the false Troyan under sail was seen,
By all the vows that ever men have broke,
In number more than ever women spoke,
In that same place thou hast appointed me,
To-morrow truly will I meet with thee.

LYSANDER
Keep promise, love. Look, here comes Helena.

Enter HELENA

HERMIA
God speed fair Helena! whither away?

HELENA
Call you me fair? that fair again unsay.
Demetrius loves your fair: O happy fair!
Your eyes are lode-stars; and your tongue's sweet air
More tuneable than lark to shepherd's ear,
When wheat is green, when hawthorn buds appear.
Sickness is catching: O, were favour so,
Yours would I catch, fair Hermia, ere I go;
My ear should catch your voice, my eye your eye,

My tongue should catch your tongue's sweet melody.
Were the world mine, Demetrius being bated,
The rest I'd give to be to you translated.
O, teach me how you look, and with what art
You sway the motion of Demetrius' heart.

HERMIA

I frown upon him, yet he loves me still.

HELENA

O that your frowns would teach my smiles such skill!

HERMIA

I give him curses, yet he gives me love.

HELENA

O that my prayers could such affection move!

HERMIA

The more I hate, the more he follows me.

HELENA

The more I love, the more he hateth me.

HERMIA

His folly, Helena, is no fault of mine.

HELENA

None, but your beauty: would that fault were mine!

HERMIA

Take comfort: he no more shall see my face;
Lysander and myself will fly this place.
Before the time I did Lysander see,
Seem'd Athens as a paradise to me:
O, then, what graces in my love do dwell,
That he hath turn'd a heaven unto a hell!

LYSANDER

Helen, to you our minds we will unfold:
To-morrow night, when Phebe doth behold
Her silver visage in the watery glass,

Decking with liquid pearl the bladed grass,
A time that lovers' flights doth still conceal,
Through Athens' gates have we devised to steal.

HERMIA
And in the wood, where often you and I
Upon faint primrose-beds were wont to lie,
Emptying our bosoms of their counsel sweet,
There my Lysander and myself shall meet;
And thence from Athens turn away our eyes,
To seek new friends and stranger companies.
Farewell, sweet playfellow: pray thou for us;
And good luck grant thee thy Demetrius!
Keep word, Lysander: we must starve our sight
From lovers' food till morrow deep midnight.

These two women are in turmoil, admittedly for different reasons, and the need to communicate their turmoil is evident in this scene which reads and plays very quickly. The rhyme scheme helps to drive the scene, keeping it moving, because Lysander and Hermia are about to fly from Athens. Helena, just coming upon the two of them, is flying too—after Demetrius, all of which is made clear after she has learned her friends' secret. Beautiful and clever rhyme, yes. But the point for these two actresses is to *pick up your cues because you are fighting to be comforted by your friend!* This will also help you avoid getting sing-songy, causing the words to sound like you are telling a dirty limerick.

You don't need to have mastered poetic meter and rhyme to play this scene. Even if you just picked up the script and had to immediately start acting it, you could do it—as long as you allow the inherent pace and accelerating rhythm of shared couplets to take hold of you. The rhyming last word, when you listen and when you follow the scene, will propel you forward. That's all you need to know! At once the scene is playing, really playing, and the audience is watching two people in sync with one another fighting to find an answer to a problem by sharing intentional rhyme at the end of every sentence. The only caution, however, would be to avoid hammering the rhyme too hard. If you find that you are doing this, first remember that rhyme wants to be said as if the character *knows* they are speaking it and *choose* to do so, and second go back to the text and if necessary write it out in prose—remember Exercise 7 instructions to help with understanding blank verse?—to keep you on point with the movement of the speech.

Now to people in love: you won't be surprised to find rhyme constantly in love scenes, when wooers are so crazy about each other they can't help finishing each other's sentences. For actors in rehearsal, it is not too great a stretch to play such moments as each lover *adding to and topping* the previous rhyme tossed to them by their beloved! I return to *Romeo and Juliet*, this time to their balcony scene in Act II, Scene 2, as Juliet quickly dashes into the house to see the Nurse:

JULIET
    A thousand times good night!

Exit, above.

ROMEO
    A thousand times the worse, to want thy light.
    Love goes toward love, as schoolboys from their books,
    But love from love, toward school with heavy looks.

You are also treated to rhyme again later when she rushes back:

JULIET
    Sweet, so would I:
    Yet I should kill thee with much cherishing.
    Good night, good night! parting is such sweet sorrow,
    That I shall say good night till it be morrow.

Exit above.

ROMEO

>Sleep dwell upon thine eyes, peace in thy breast!
>Would I were sleep and peace, so sweet to rest!
>Hence will I to my ghostly father's cell,
>His help to crave, and my dear hap to tell.

You witness this in a different way when Romeo goes to his confessor Friar Laurence to tell him of his new-found love. This scene drives just as much—or at least it should—propelled by just as much need, but it is between two men, a young man and an older man who is his mentor. Romeo is ecstatically divulging his glorious secret; Friar Laurence is blown away by the news and immediately fights to get the young man to calm down and talk sense:

FRIAR LAURENCE

>... What early tongue so sweet saluteth me?
>Young son, it argues a distemper'd head
>So soon to bid good morrow to thy bed:
>Care keeps his watch in every old man's eye,
>And where care lodges, sleep will never lie;
>But where unbruised youth with unstuff'd brain
>Doth couch his limbs, there golden sleep doth reign:
>Therefore thy earliness doth me assure
>Thou art up-roused by some distemperature;
>Or if not so, then here I hit it right,
>Our Romeo hath not been in bed to-night.

ROMEO

>That last is true; the sweeter rest was mine.

FRIAR LAURENCE

>God pardon sin! wast thou with Rosaline?

ROMEO

>With Rosaline, my ghostly father? no;
>I have forgot that name, and that name's woe.

FRIAR LAURENCE
That's my good son: but where hast thou been, then?

ROMEO
I'll tell thee, ere thou ask it me again.
I have been feasting with mine enemy,
Where on a sudden one hath wounded me,
That's by me wounded: both our remedies
Within thy help and holy physic lies:
I bear no hatred, blessed man, for, lo,
My intercession likewise steads my foe.

FRIAR LAURENCE
Be plain, good son, and homely in thy drift;
Riddling confession finds but riddling shrift.

ROMEO
Then plainly know my heart's dear love is set
On the fair daughter of rich Capulet:
As mine on hers, so hers is set on mine;
And all combined, save what thou must combine
By holy marriage: when and where and how
We met, we woo'd and made exchange of vow,
I'll tell thee as we pass; but this I pray,
That thou consent to marry us to-day.

FRIAR LAURENCE
Holy Saint Francis, what a change is here!
Is Rosaline, whom thou didst love so dear,
So soon forsaken? young men's love then lies
Not truly in their hearts, but in their eyes.
Jesu Maria, what a deal of brine
Hath wash'd thy sallow cheeks for Rosaline!
How much salt water thrown away in waste,
To season love, that of it doth not taste!
The sun not yet thy sighs from heaven clears,
Thy old groans ring yet in my ancient ears;
Lo, here upon thy cheek the stain doth sit

Of an old tear that is not wash'd off yet:
If e'er thou wast thyself and these woes thine,
Thou and these woes were all for Rosaline:
And art thou changed? pronounce this sentence then,
Women may fall, when there's no strength in men.

ROMEO
Thou chid'st me oft for loving Rosaline.

FRIAR LAURENCE
For doting, not for loving, pupil mine.

ROMEO
And bad'st me bury love.

FRIAR LAURENCE
Not in a grave,
To lay one in, another out to have.

ROMEO
I pray thee, chide not; she whom I love now
Doth grace for grace and love for love allow;
The other did not so.

FRIAR LAURENCE
O, she knew well
Thy love did read by rote and could not spell.
But come, young waverer, come, go with me,
In one respect I'll thy assistant be;
For this alliance may so happy prove,
To turn your households' rancour to pure love.

ROMEO
O, let us hence; I stand on sudden haste.

FRIAR LAURENCE
Wisely and slow; they stumble that run fast.

Exeunt.

You will also find couplets binding people together out of hatred or strife, as in *Othello*. First, in Act I, Scene 3, when the Duke of Venice tries to calm Brabantio:

> . . . And, noble signior,
> If virtue no delighted beauty lack,
> Your son-in-law is far more fair than black.

The Duke exits after completing this line. Before he himself exits, Brabantio cannot resist one last warning—and *prophesy*—to the Moor:

> Look to her, Moor, if thou hast eyes to see:
> She has deceived her father, and may thee.

It can be both to let the audience know the present scene is ending but "hang on, something big is going to happen!" *and* it can be between two people in tremendous need of each other—thrown together by love or hate—who cannot resist completing or carrying on each other's sentences. In addition, historically, couplets were employed for other reasons, such as to help off-stage actors to hear their entrance cue for the following scene, an unabashed prompting for the audience to applaud, or Shakespeare's stage direction to an actor that they must perform a false exit and then return to speak another thought.

As you work on a scene or monologue with rhyme spoken by a character—and I assure you that I am not the first one to dream this up—know that your character is doing so *on purpose to get something*. Got it? 'Nuff said.

Sonnets

A sonnet is a 14-line poem that expresses a single thought. It is written in iambic pentameter, and the 14 lines are divided up into three four-line sections called *quatrains*. Quatrains are four lines of verse that make up a stanza. The three quatrains are labeled first, second, and third quatrain. The final two lines of the sonnet are in the form of a rhyme couplet. The idea of the poem is expressed in this order:

First quatrain: expresses the overall theme of the poem.
Second quatrain: the theme is explained in greater detail.
Third quatrain: expresses some conflict in the heart of the writer, often begun with the word "but." To impress your friends you can let them know that this conflict is also called *peripeteia*.
Couplet: concludes the sonnet by summing up its overall theme.

Shakespeare wrote 154 sonnets, perhaps between 1592 and 1598. Most of them (126) are written to a young man; the remaining 28 (127–154) are written to an ominous, unknown woman referred to as the "dark lady." Without Shakespeare's permission the sonnets were published in quarto form in 1609, along with his longer poem *The Passionate Pilgrim*. Because so many of them were devoted to a young man it has been theorized that Shakespeare was gay and he wrote them to proclaim his love for, perhaps, William Herbert, Earl of Pembroke (one of the people to whom the inaugural First Folio edition was dedicated as "most noble and incomparable brethren"), though we do not know this for a certainty. In this same whispered theory we must also mention Henry Wriothesley, 3rd Earl of Southampton, a valued patron to whom Shakespeare dedicated *Venus and Adonis* and *The Rape of Lucrece*. To be fair, however, it must be pointed out that in Elizabethan times men often expressed their great friendship for one another in terms of "love."

We have touched on how Shakespeare uses his verse to help his actors play fright and urgency through sharing lines, how he helps them let the audience know that something big is going to happen soon through the capping couplet, and how he inserts rhyme willy-nilly into scenes to make his characters raise the stakes, whether out of distress or joy. But in *Romeo and Juliet*, his greatest love story, he goes a step farther in Act I, Scene 5, providing the two teenagers a scene in which they not only share lines to show their growing instant love, he also builds the driving chemistry between them by making their first meeting—a back-and-forth conversation you might call playful sparring—into a *sonnet*:

ROMEO
>If I profane with my unworthiest hand
>This holy shrine, the gentle fine is this:
>My lips, two blushing pilgrims, ready stand
>To smooth that rough touch with a tender kiss.

JULIET
>Good pilgrim, you do wrong your hand too much,
>Which mannerly devotion shows in this;
>For saints have hands that pilgrims' hands do touch,
>And palm to palm is holy palmers' kiss.

ROMEO
>Have not saints lips, and holy palmers too?

JULIET
>Ay, pilgrim, lips that they must use in prayer.

ROMEO
>O, then, dear saint, let lips do what hands do;
>They pray, grant thou, lest faith turn to despair.

JULIET
>Saints do not move, though grant for prayers' sake.

ROMEO
>Then move not, while my prayer's effect I take.

You don't need to be some great acting teacher to see that here you have two young folks that are instantly in love, and they are rejoicing in wordplay with each other for the first time. It is the kind of fun that can only lead—which it of course does—to their first kiss! Young actors, that's all you have to do to play this scene! These two kids *dig* each other, and are having the time of their young lives building up to a kiss they both know is coming! Girls, if you know what it's like to feel that a guy is cute, you can play this scene; boys, if you remember what came to your mind when you saw a lady across the room you thought was hot, you can play this scene—it is as simple as that! Acting Shakespeare might be outrageous but it is not rocket science!

Exercise 21: Write a Sonnet

In Exercise 9 you took a blank verse speech apart by writing it all out in prose. Now let's go in the other direction by having you write your *own sonnet*. It's okay; don't be scared. It'll be fun. I recommend you start by studying one of Shakespeare's most famous sonnets, such as Sonnet 18, "Shall I compare thee to a summer's day . . . ?" Just try to be as strict as you can with the rhythm and make sure it is the standard 14 lines ending in a rhyme couplet. To put my money where my mouth is—and because I trust that you won't throw tomatoes at me (although I won't blame you if you do)—I have included below a little sonnet of my own for you to look at. The one you write can be about any old thing; as lofty—or, in my case, as frivolous—as you choose to make it. The point is that you are in the *action* of making Shakespeare's use of words your *own*:

> When I do knead the dough so rough and hard
> And set the oven temp so full and high,
> I bounce and roll the flour half a yard,
> To bake a cake that rises to the sky.
> Your birthday party leads me ever strong,
> To make your gift so tasty and so sweet
> That you enjoy its taste full all night long,
> 'Till dawn itself your lovely eyes do greet.
> But any cake is poor when next to you,
> Sugar stale in battle with your lips,
> And pies and doughnuts also will not do,

All bowing to the beauty of your hips.
Your love is icing on an angel cake
Far greater than my careful hands could bake.

Most often Shakespeare's sonnets are in the form of melancholy pleas. He continues to surprise us by doing the unexpected and out of the ordinary—the outrageous—by using this particular poetic form to show everlasting love at first sight. This is exactly what the actors want to play in acting this beautiful scene. They are best avoided as audition material, however, because they are not inherently active or driven in a scene that is one-on-one, or that demands that characters get something from someone right now.

* * *

Think of blank verse in these ways:

1. to portray the rich, high-born and learned;
2. to portray characters speaking to one another with love;
3. to portray heightened need no matter what the social status.

Prose: How *We* Talk

This is the second form of language you will most often see in Shakespeare. You will know it because it is simply laid out like the pages of a book; left to right printing with no obvious pattern of stress or non-stress, and the letters are not capitalized on the left-hand side. Shakespeare most often used prose for his characters of the lower class—servants, laborers, etc.—but he did not limit it to them. Both upper- and lower-class characters speak prose from time to time. It all has to do with expressing the desires of their heart. As I have previously mentioned, Shakespeare has King Henry V speak prose with great dexterity to his soldiers in the campfire scenes, but in *Henry IV, Part 1* Prince Hal goes back and forth between courtly iambic pentameter and country prose with Falstaff. Conversely, as we have shown, lower class such as Silvius and Phebe speak poetry in their "love" scene in *As You Like It*. Think of iambic pentameter as heightened language for *specific effect and weighty need*. Consider prose in these two ways:

1. to portray common, simple folk;
2. to allow the character, whatever their station in life, *to speak their mind with greater plainness*, such as private scenes in which they are plotting evil or fun.

Prose is spoken when the character does not have the "soft phrase of peace," either from being uneducated or underprivileged and therefore forced by circumstance to not mince words. You also find it spoken by cynical, plain-speaking wits offering commentary on the world around them (Jaques and Touchstone, both in *As You Like It*). In addition, Shakespeare employs prose in exposition, letters, and proclamations, speeches spoken out of madness whether pretended or real (think of Hamlet and Lady Macbeth), and for low comedy scenes (think the rude mechanicals in *A Midsummer Night's Dream* and *The Comedy of Errors*).

Here is a moving example of plain speaking, from *Henry V*, in which Mistress Quickly (in this play referred to as "Hostess") speaks of the death of Sir John Falstaff:

> Nay, sure, he's not in hell: he's in Arthur's bosom, if ever man went to Arthur's bosom. A' made a finer end and went away an it had been any christom child; a' parted even just between twelve and one, even at the turning o' the tide: for after I saw him fumble with the sheets and play with flowers and smile upon his fingers' ends, I knew there was but one way; for his nose was as sharp as a pen, and a' babbled of green

fields. "How now, sir John!" quoth I. "What, man! be o' good cheer." So a' cried out "God, God, God!" three or four times. Now I, to comfort him, bid him a' should not think of God; I hoped there was no need to trouble himself with any such thoughts yet. So a' bade me lay more clothes on his feet: I put my hand into the bed and felt them, and they were as cold as any stone; then I felt to his knees, and they were as cold as any stone, and so upward and upward, and all was as cold as any stone.

Without any trouble at all the actress playing this role can easily inform—and *move*—the audience, by simply playing the scene and speaking the lines. One of our best examples of this is Dame Judi Dench's reading in Kenneth Branagh's fine film of the play. But you can do it, too, just by memorizing the words, and *doing it* . . .

Dag-nabbit! Shakespeare's Made-up Words

As vivid as Shakespeare's words had to be, even he got stuck once and a while searching for the right words to convey what he was trying to say. So you know what he did? He just *made up* words to help him. How many did he make up? Various figures have been postulated, but what seems to be the most prevalent estimation is that Shakespeare created some 1700 words for this purpose; but don't get nervous, because you will be speaking sounds that can only be explained by scholarly notes at the bottom of the page. These made-up words would have baffled the Elizabethan audience the first time they heard them, too. When speaking these bizarre sounds it is vital that they be played to the very hilt, *especially* if you don't know what you are saying. How do you think we came up with the likes of our own unique expletives? Such nonsense words come out of you because your desire to communicate is so great that, in the face of the appropriate word eluding you, you knew that you just had to go ahead and speak anyway, you *needed* to speak anyway! When you accidentally bang your finger or stub your toe or get so frazzled by a sudden life reversal you don't know what to say and yet you know that something *must* be said out loud to express your displeasure! You wind up shouting, "Fudge!" instead of a certain other word beginning with f, or yelling "S...t!" or even "Dag-nabbit!" if you dropped something on your foot. What in the world does "Dag-nabbit" mean? Other than to *express the inexpressible when expression is a must*!

Shakespeare knew this too. The only difference—other than his genius—is that he had a 400-plus-year head start. Language, as you know, is always evolving—you merely have to take a gander at Webster's Dictionary to see the words and phrases now considered commonplace after being shunned generations ago, many of which (like the uncountable additions to Webster's over the generations) we now have come to know as commonplace. Consider these, from Chapter 3 of *The Shakespeare Book of Lists*:

> advertising, bandit, critic, dickens, epileptic, film, gossip, hush, investment, jig, kissing, luggage, manager, numb, obscene, puke, quarrelsome, rant, shooting star, torture, undress, varied, wild-goose chase, yelping, zany.

Yes, sir, we believe most if not all of the above were concocted by Shakespeare, or at least were part of the common cultural vernacular and it was he who first put them down in print (such as the example "zany" above, which comes from *zanni*, first appearing in *commedia dell'arte*). But mostly likely he also made up words that would be unique to the language of his own time (remember your own present-day "dag-nabbit"). Here, along with their meaning, are a few of them, also from *The Shakespeare Book of Lists*:

> addition—title
> alarum—call to arms with trumpets
> aroint—begone

ACT THREE: WORDS, WORDS, WORDS!

baffle (which for our purposes has come to mean "to confuse")—to hang up a person by the heels as a mark of disgrace
balk (remember a baseball pitcher who hesitates at the wrong time?)—to disregard
belike—maybe
bum (still today, spoken mostly by the British)—backside, buttocks
character—handwriting
dispatch—to hurry
enow—enough
fare-thee-well (even today)—goodbye
fustian—wretched
honest—chaste, pure
list—listen
morrow—day
power—army
recreant—coward
stale—harlot
tax—to criticize, to accuse
want—lack
wherefore—why
zounds—by his [Christ's] wounds.

And, yet again from *Lists*, some that are even more obscure, along the lines of our own colloquial "old fuddy-duddy," "horn-swaggled," "bam-boozled," etc.:

a-birding—hunting small birds
ambuscado—ambush
boiled-brains—hot-headed youths
brabbler—quarreler
canker-blossom—worm in the bud
clapper-claw—to thrash or maul
dewlap—loose skin at the throat
dotard—old fool

fancy-monger—a lovesick man
fardel—burden
geck—fool
gibbet—gallows
hugger-mugger—secrecy
logger-headed—stupid
maltworm—heavy drinker
noddy—simpleton
periwig-pated—bewigged
poop (not what you think)—infect with venereal disease
reechy—grimy
skains-mate—criminal
skimble-skamble—nonsensical
slug-a-bed—sleepyhead
thwack—drive away
welkin—sky
whirligig—a top

These strange and wonderful words share a very common thing: they require your full, open, articulated mouth and lips to properly do justice to them (warm up your lips and tongue!). You must hit consonants with great force, you must allow your mouth to open wide for a vowel—in short you must deliver them as someone who *must speak but has no other word to use but this one*! You certainly recall (from Exercise 14 in Act Two) the kind of energy and punch exerted when driven to shout, "F...k!" This is how you must deliver all the "Shakespearean" words our twenty-first-century ears are not accustomed to hearing, and especially those words made up in the desperation of human need.

* * *

The language of the New Millennium is still evolving, too, just as much as, if not more so than, in Shakespeare's time. Look at these more recent examples of made-up words from Merriam-Webster's Open Dictionary online:

agnostophobia *(noun)*: fear of the unknown
benies *(noun)*: benefits
cutieful *(adjective)*: beautiful and cute
dope *(adjective)*: very good: excellent
gratisfaction *(noun)*: gratitude and satisfaction
malware *(noun)*: a dangerous virus that can destroy your computer's functionality.
popemobile *(noun)*: the special vehicle that transports the Pope in public appearances
wackadoodle *(adjective)*: not quite right: wackier than wacky

Are these words any wilder, more unique to our society and the world in which we live and hope to thrive than the vast array of nouns, verbs, and adjectives penned by William Shakespeare? In addition, they are examples of words created by many people and used in popular culture, not only penned by the Bard of Avon alone. To keep jogging your memory I have included a longer list of his more frequently used words in the Glossary in the back of this book.

Summary

1. Follow Shakespeare's punctuation.
2. The use of *thee* and *thou* is about human relationship and need.
3. Blank verse is heightened need but not just about being high-born.
4. Iambic pentameter helps you memorize your words.
5. Shared lines are telling you to pick up the cues.
6. Rhyme verse is speaking out of great need to make a point.
7. Prose is about plain speaking as well as being poor.
8. Both upper- and lower-class characters speak prose.
9. Both upper- and lower-class characters speak verse.

10. Feminine endings are about actively trying to solve a problem.
11. Long descriptive passages help you to build emotion.
12. Characters make up words out of an outrageous need to speak.

Act Four

DIVERS SCHEDULES

A Few Items Picked Up Watching Actors Do Shakespeare

> O, sir, I will not be so hard-hearted; I will give out divers schedules of my beauty: it shall be inventoried, and every particle and utensil labelled to my will: as, item, two lips, indifferent red; item, two grey eyes, with lids to them; item, one neck, one chin, and so forth. Were you sent hither to praise me?
>
> (Olivia in Twelfth Night)

In all the years that I have been an actor I have had the good fortune to act in many of Shakespeare's plays. Even better, I have been able to watch other actors perform him and hear fine directors and teachers explain him. I have included a few of the items here, observations which have come to me from watching as well as from personal experience, during those precious moments either in rehearsal or after the show over drinks when we were unable to resist sharing what we had just learned in our journey of "doing Shakespeare."

Item 1: There is No Subtext in Shakespeare

The more you study the words for clues on how to act his plays, the more likely it will be that you might one day be moved to ask yourself, "Is there *subtext* in Shakespeare?" You may even have marvelous friendly arguments about this subject; the idea that, in the end, substantively, in the plays of William Shakespeare there is no presence of *subtext*. In speaking about this with your friends you will tussle over just what is the motivation driving Iago, or Edmund the Bastard in *King Lear*, or Don John the Bastard in *Much Ado About Nothing*, or Richard III gleefully toppling all of his enemies, even Mistress Page and Mistress Ford conniving to get even with Sir John Falstaff in *The Merry Wives of Windsor*. Soon, after so much good-natured sparring, you will probably discover what was getting between you in the first place; it is entirely possible you were arguing over *semantics*. The more you talk the more it becomes clear that you did not necessarily disagree with your friends; in fact you were actually speaking and agreeing upon the same things. You were saying toe-*may*-toes while they were saying toe-*mah*-toes. So, gratefully, you arrive at a definition of the *context* of what you were proposing, and it becomes possible for you and your friends to finally agree on at least a few points:

1. Shakespeare's characters tell *willful lies* to other characters.
2. Shakespeare's characters deliberately *hold back* vital information from other characters knowing full well that to do so will create confusion and perhaps distress in the heart of the hearer.
3. Shakespeare's characters address their fellow characters with *ulterior motives* meant to bring about harm or joy to the hearer (as the lying plotting friends help Beatrice and Benedick fall in love with one another or Iago duping Rodrigo, Cassio, and Othello).
4. *But*, at the same time, Shakespeare's characters will tell *you* in the audience exactly what they are about to do *before* they do it. At every turn, whether aside, monologue, or soliloquy, they express their true thoughts to you.

I suppose there are some of you who might claim this qualifies as subtext. I say that it qualifies as *guile*, and what's more, guile that is not hidden or secret, but that which is actively sought out to be shared with someone—and not just you in the audience—

at the earliest opportunity. Merriam Webster states that guile is "the use of clever and usually dishonest methods to achieve something." It is deceitful, it is cunning, it is calculating. *But it is not subtext because they do not keep from the audience the fact that they are being dishonest.* They do not even keep it from themselves, for even if ostensibly they are speaking directly to the audience they are ruminating out loud when they happen to be alone. However, if you choose to call the above subtext I can't stop you.

On the other hand, it might be that some of you are speaking of subtext as we have come to know it in the American acting tradition: more complex and weighty, a hidden agenda that is *implied* by a character but not necessarily *stated* by that character in the dialogue; you might be saying that it must be rooted out of the events of the play because it is believed that somehow, *somewhere*, it is locked in the heart of the character even though it is never actually *spoken* by that character!

In this case I insist we are speaking of apples and oranges because we are talking about play structures as different as night and day. *Our* modern-day subtext is based on what, over time, we have evolved it to mean from the work of Konstantin Stanislavsky—information in a play that is inherently buried in some "other where" (as Shakespeare might call it) than in the text. We had help getting to this notion, of course, with the work of the "well-made play" by Henrik Ibsen, modern drama by Anton Chekhov, naturalism by August Strindberg, and later when it was further realized by Lillian Hellman and Lanford Wilson and many others in contemporary drama. Also don't forget that famed acting teacher Lee Strasberg did his bit with his own deconstruction of Stanislavsky, which led to Strasberg's reimagining of the Russian director's work eventually being called "The Method." I get all of that. I agree that, in the above examples of how plays have come to be written during the last 400-plus years, this iteration of subtext is alive and well and ripe for the digging.

But, by now certainly, you know that Shakespeare's characters —as well as those created by the playwrights of his time—are written differently. His people say what they mean and they mean what they say. The character may be consciously keeping something *from* another character or even lying to them, but they do not hold this close to their vest; they tell *you* that they have just done so and that they will continue to do so and then they tell *you* why. Nothing is hidden from you. Their motive for doing what they do is spoken to you "in private," when they are alone on stage or they choose to turn to you in an aside. Shakespeare's characters *tell the listeners what they are about to do*. In addition to spouting poetry that soared farther above the heights than any other dramatist ever had before him or since him, Shakespeare's plays also, at face value, are stories being *told by the actors*.

Storytellers today might occasionally get cute by keeping little tidbits of information from their audience as a means of building suspense for some great "surprise ending" to their tales for dramatic effect, but Shakespeare's characters do not do this. His plays are constructed so that the characters can feel deeply and wail at their own tragedy or joy in their happiness at the *same time* they are telling *you* what will happen next. Subtext as we theatrical types have come to know it centuries later is different from these plays in no small part because of the production wherewithal Shakespeare had and did not have. I remind you again his plays were performed at two o'clock each afternoon on a wooden stage with a hole in the roof in front of as many as 3000 people. Shakespeare had no newspapers, no radio, no television, no internet, few available books, and no spectator sport more otherwise lofty than bear-baiting or hanging. The one arguable exception was in the case of costumes, regulated by the English Sumptuary Law of 1574 (The Statutes of Revels).[1] Through this law, actors were able to have expensive ornate costumes while at the same time possessing precious few props. In text, not only did a character's desires have to be made clear but also a vivid picture had to be painted of the time of day, the dark of night, the sound of cannons and the thunder of horses' hooves and the height of love and depth of hate and much more. The Elizabethans had for family entertainment stories that had been handed down from legend over generations, and—most important of all—because of this they had reverence for the spoken word. This society must have certainly inspired the term "hear a play," and going to the theatre was for them what going to movies and rock concerts and sporting events is for us. In telling stories (presenting plays) in the Elizabethan tradition it would have been anathema for a character to hold back from their audience; if it exists, Shakespeare's only "subtext" consisted of that which is *hidden from character to character*, but even then he lets *you* in on it.

Now, admittedly, this does have a limit: once his villainous characters have done their deed he will then silence them from speaking directly to the audience for the rest of the play. It may be he did this because his villains needed to become less your confidant and more of a bad guy soon to be dead, so he would no longer allow them to get all chummy by speaking directly to you. Some of the instances he does this is in the case of Richard III, Edmund the Bastard in *King Lear*, and Iago. After more than two hours' traffic on the stage they suddenly seem to clam up. For the better part of the play these villains establish a nice little folksy relationship with the audience, then suddenly—poof! You are cut off from their private confessions, not long before they are given their just desserts.

What This Means for Your Acting

But don't miss my point: I am not saying all this to add academic rumination to the endless minutiae of Shakespearean discussion. What I mean is this: no subtext in Shakespeare means your acting must be about *doing!*

Item 2: There is Never a "Fourth Wall"

The "Fourth Wall," that black abyss into which actors look to open themselves up to the audience on a proscenium stage, is about presentation, establishing a conceit and accepted reality which the acting company wants to keep behind a curtain or at least disguised from the eye of the audience lest the ability to believe in the play would be irreparably damaged. You might say it is about keeping hidden. Shakespeare's plays had no "Fourth Wall" because they were never performed on a proscenium stage in his lifetime, and this had a lot to do with how he wrote and how his plays were presented. But no such desire to hide is present in Shakespearean performance, and you must remember all of this as you attempt his words *today*; you must consider yourself always on display, always seen even if you cannot see the audience, always visible in body as well as voice, always observed when not even speaking. Film acting—which so many young actors are drawn to today—did not exist and would not have even been a dream. Your presentation must therefore be alive and observed, as nakedly exposed. Every character you play must feel this way and this must infuse their very words. You must accept the notion that you will always be showing "back" to someone, and not just because the stage would have been configured into the shape of a thrust; you must realize that you are always listening, alert, alive, "*in* the scene," "in the *moment*," and the "back" you turn to them must be active, as well—I am serious—the muscles of your shoulder blades and spine pulsing with your every utterance and discovery as a Shakespearean character. Never forget this as you speak aloud the stories being told by William Shakespeare, even if you are acting on a stage that *has* a fourth wall.

What This Means for Your Acting

The presentational nature of not having a fourth wall opens up your performance to be shared better by the audience; it is not about being bombastic and loud. It is about being honest and true—to everyone within the sound of your voice. In addition, when first experienced by Shakespeare's actors, it was a necessity rather than a mere acting choice to be more "open" so as to be seen; the house of spectators eventually, unruly as they were, would not take too kindly if they missed action and words for too long because an actor seemed to be shunning them. They might decide to start throwing things. But for us today—for *you*—take this note as a way to find greater more aggressive need in your character to *exist*, to fight for what they want in the scene and the play.

Item 3: Size is About More than Being Big and Loud

Now, you live in the twenty-first century. You have all the technological, educational, and cultural benefits William Shakespeare did not. You might not get the chance to perform him outdoors in an amphitheater or on the boards of the Globe or even indoors theater at the Blackfriars; you will probably work on a normal proscenium stage or indoor thrust stage or in-the-round black box; you will benefit from indoor lighting, safe from the unreliable elements of rain or snow or cold; you will have electrical stage lighting to aid you as you speak about the dark of night or the bright of day or even the torrent of rain. In the auditorium the lights will go out to help your audience along with the "willing suspension of disbelief" that they are traveling somewhere far away for the next two or three hours. You have all of these things as helpmeets. The one thing necessary to add to your performance will be *size*, but this size is about more than just being big and loud, and in most cases it won't be about those things at all.

Shakespeare's world and culture demanded that his plays be performed a certain way but it is the genius of his themes and language that catapulted them past the footlights. In other words, yes, if you spoke before a few thousand people who could all see you it would have been necessary to speak loudly and clearly enough for them to hear you—but what made them listen and what engaged them is what Shakespeare chose to infuse into his words, his choices of poetry or prose and his decision to break the rules of both, and his brilliant creation of words and phrases to express himself. Shakespeare's words possess size because of the weight of his *themes* as well as his genius, and your performance must be driven by those themes. You are not speaking words from a television situation comedy or episodic drama—though many of these are in their own way brilliant and far-reaching. Shakespeare plays are not film scripts; they are theatrical blueprints, and the size required of them, both physical as well as thematic, will work whether the venue is a 2000 seat theater or a 150-seat black box space, because this size is not about being loud—though you sometimes may need to be—it is about being *clear* and understood by the hearer, and that comes from making his words your own. Whatever the venue, Shakespeare must be heard clearly in order to be understood because the visual clues we gain from movies today are not there—they are drawn in broad strokes by the words. This is another reason why the question of subtext in Shakespeare is not a certain one; the structure of his plays is about *telling you a story*; how can you visualize his tale if he is willfully keeping something from you? Young actors desirous of being "real" try too often to whisper and mumble text that was never meant to be whispered or mumbled, even at its softest.

What This Means for Your Acting

Even in the smallest theater space you must speak Shakespeare clearly and forcefully, with as much dynamism as can aid your lips to paint a picture and your lungs to support the sound rushing by those lips. Because your needs are farther away from you than the space separating you from the audience. You begin by making those words simply and honestly your *own*.

Item 4: Play What the Scene is *Doing*—Not Just What the Words Mean

Sometimes actors work so hard at "making sense" of the Shakespeare text they are working on they forget that the scene must also be about simple human relationships. I have seen this happen in many Shakespeare productions, but one that stands out in my mind is what I witnessed once in a production of *Macbeth* in Act IV, Scene 3, the long scene between Macduff, Malcolm, and Ross. If you're not careful this scene becomes an exhausting rhetorical debate on how to govern a kingdom—a debate at a podium, mind you; not a human struggle fraught with conflict. In all, 158 lines are spoken, with the very brief entrance and exit of the Doctor, before Ross even enters with what will be bad news; this should be a clue to the actor that a conversation of *some* considerable import is going on. But what is going on, and what, once the actor understands the meaning of the words, is the scene about? What can we say that the scene is *doing*? And don't think that I am getting all "subtextually" about it. Listen to the words Shakespeare begins the scene with, spoken by Malcolm:

> Let us seek out some desolate shade, and there
> Weep our sad bosoms empty.

Take these words literally, for what they mean on their face. Think of what has happened, and it is from the text: Macduff and Malcolm are on the run. Malcolm is running because he thinks he'll be blamed for his father Duncan's murder, and Macduff is running because he's afraid that Macbeth's long knives might be pointed at him. They both are on the run. They *do not have the time* to stop in a private patch of the countryside for an intellectual conversation; they are desperately making their way toward England, where there are armed forces sympathetic to their cause. They are stopping to weep their "sad bosoms empty." Actors in rehearsal can ask themselves how many days they have traveled, how many nights they have missed sleep, how many nightmares Malcolm has had about the horrific murder of his father, how many images of abandoned wife and babes have kept Macduff awake. It can be asked, how much water do they have? How much food? Are their horses fresh? Are they on foot? What does Macduff think of Malcolm? Perhaps he blames the kid for the king's death, or maybe he looks down on Malcolm for running away? In the scene it also comes up that Malcolm is a virgin; could he be jealous of Macduff because the older man has had sex before? Does he look down on Macduff for abandoning his beautiful wife and children?

These questions are fair game for actors rehearsing the scene for performance, and they are all rooted in the text. It is not an exaggeration to suggest that the scene wants to be contentious, an *argument*, always on the brink of a knock-down drag-out fight. Any theatre company "putting on a show" for an audience can rightfully want what is going to be most active for their paying customers. Perhaps the two men are close to drawing weapons— or better yet, *have* drawn weapons—just as Ross enters. Many words are spoken in the text before Macduff finds out about his family's slaughter; playing the scene should not be a demonstration of how much sense the actors can make of the text; rather, in speaking that text the actors should make it clear *how reasonable men are driven to unreasonable actions because of war*, and of course I would ask that you substitute "unreasonable" for *outrageous*. One man is guilt-ridden over being a coward (Macduff) and the younger man (Malcolm) is guilty of being exposed as a mere boy who cannot even make love to a woman, let alone rule a kingdom or mastermind a coup against his own father. During the scene accusations ought to be made, the two of them must fly off the handle; they must come close to saying things to one another that cannot be taken back—all because of the personal turmoil and guilt coursing through them. They do not need to like one another—at least not *yet*; it is often in the midst of the most spiteful disagreement that men are able to grudgingly respect one another and become friends. Suppose, for the sake of theatricality, Macduff is on the verge of cutting Malcolm's throat but stops short because he finally sees some hope in the young man—and it is then that Ross enters and Macduff is told of the horror visited upon his deserted household?

And even then; after that moment of unspeakable grief, why not have them go after one another again with blood in their eyes? This time because Malcolm has chided Macduff to "Dispute it like a man!" How about that? This kid still wet behind the ears telling Macduff how to grieve for his newly murdered wife and babies? Would not that cause a reasonable man, a warrior, to go after someone with the intent to kill? Ross can be forced to separate them! Then, catching their breath, Macduff can realize that his quarrel is actually with Macbeth and not Malcolm nor Ross. Macduff finally is able to collect himself—his anger as well as tears are able to subside—and he can see clearly that the three of them are actually allies and they must continue on to England, where they can finish raising their army.

Yes, I have just gone through scene choices that a director might use to liven up a slow-moving reading of the scene (cuts can be made, but you can't cut the entire scene). I admit that. But I challenge that the interpretation is inspired by the words and action of the scene. Is not this a much more interesting take on the scene than what it can become when actors approaching Shakespeare's text sometimes fall prey to—making "sense" of the text? The text is still made ample sense of, the words still clear, even more so because the audience is helped to understand what is going on *viscerally* between these two men.

Use the outrageous situation caused by love the characters have been placed in, and play the even more outrageous words and made-up words the playwright has given you. But remember the meaning of these words is always active, not scholarly. *Scholars* have made Shakespeare scholarly, not the man himself.

What This Means for Your Acting

Please make sense of the text and understand what you are saying. But that is only half of the actor's job; in playing a scene in front of an audience, remember that it is not an intellectual exercise: it is an *entertainment,* in the form of live theatre, meant to depict human beings fighting with each other—whether in love or in hate—as they struggle to stay alive in a world that is unfair. In working on your role you are after not only what the words merely mean, you are after what has driven you to say them in the first place!

Item 5: Antithesis is Fighting for an Answer by Comparing Opposites

Play the *antithesis* of the speech. This is how Shakespeare was able to create characters of depth and humanity with the words. By balancing imagery between opposites, hot and cold, white and black, day and night, etc., he was able to present human beings who actually did not have all the answers, who questioned their very existence, who were not certain of what even they themselves held to be absolute truth because there *was no* absolute truth. When you see Shakespeare make these comparisons in the text, play them extra hard because you can bet the character is asking for an answer out loud to a question that has troubled fallible human beings for all time. Have you ever left someone after yelling at them, saying, "Why did I do that? That's not like me!" We flawed race of people are constantly doing the opposite of what we intend to do, going against what we proclaim ourselves assured of, even being guilty of behaving like we don't believe we are capable of behaving. Shakespeare is constantly comparing opposites, even in joyous frivolous moments, such as when Theseus says of the Pyramus and Thisbe play, "That is hot ice and wondrous strange snow." He also does this when a character speaks of love and hate in the same sentence. Setting the word against the word to help the audience gain context is perhaps Shakespeare's greatest tool, and it will enrich your performance as well.

What This Means for Your Acting

It can be said that antithesis is fighting for an answer to a crucial problem—by *comparing the choices*. And of course you know that the greatest example of this in his work is when Hamlet thinks out loud, "To be, or not to be."

Exercise 22: Play the Antithesis

This exercise is about playing antithesis, setting the word against the word. Take an antithetical line from a Shakespeare speech (they are plentiful; you won't have any trouble finding them).

You might try these. I have indicated the comparisons in **bold**:

Come, Montague, for thou art early **up**
To see thy son and heir now early **down**.

I will be **brief**, for my short date of breath
Is not so **long** as is a tedious tale.

Fair is **foul**, and foul is **fair**. . .

What he has **lost**, noble Macbeth has **won**. . .

Who wooed in **haste** and means to wed at **leisure**.

Come, **night**; end, **day**.

Give every man thy **ear**, but few thy **voice**.

And, of course:

To **be**, or **not** to **be**.

This can be done in class. Teacher can print out examples on single strips of paper and each student will draw one from a hat. To play the game each student will rise when chosen and proclaim aloud the two words of their antithetical line, each *differently*. Listed below are possibilities to try. The first choice you see is for the first word, the second for the second word (but you can certainly switch the order in any way that you like):

Shout	Whisper
Lie down	Spring up
Advance	Retreat
Laugh	Cry
Sing	Stutter
Staccato	Legato
Thrust (with a sword)	Parry
Attack	Surrender
Reach for the sky	Grovel on the ground

Each time, try to sense the difference in the *sound* and *rhythm* of the word one from the other, then speak the line in context, as a character might to contrast them by comparison.

- Why does the character make this comparison?
- What point are they trying to make?
- Continue the exercise, practicing with objects, places, things, etc., such as:

Dog	Cat
Hero	Villain
Rain	Sun
Dark	Light
This	That

Continue to experiment with the sound and how you can make each word different by varying the sound, pitch, or rhythm. You can even do a variation on the improv similar to Exercise 20, "Dueling Shakespeare." Each student, with opposite words, can "duel" each other, trying with their "quick draw" to *top* the other. Then perform the passage without the exercise to see how it affects your understanding of setting the word against the word.

Item 6: Don't Report, Make a *Discovery*!

I am forever astounded that, when I ask a young acting student what he or she wants in the scene, they will say, "To get information."

What is just as tricky is the Shakespearean speech, usually long, which appears at first glance to be merely about reporting information or providing exposition.

Exposition must not be played like exposition.

The long descriptive speeches—such as Friar Laurence's page-long "I will be brief" final speech from Act V, Scene 3 in *Romeo and Juliet*—are not about reporting what has happened, even though on the face of it that may be what they are doing. At the end of the friar's long confession he offers up his "old life" to be sacrificed to "severest law." The friar is not recounting what he witnessed and the part he played in it; he is giving a *confession*, as for absolution, for sins he committed against God and the state. Such monologues should be active, driven, aggressive *battles* to win certainty and comfort in the life of the speaker. This is also true of messenger and servant characters, given short shrift by having to wait so long off stage and required to perform yeoman's duty when back on. Of these the best, most challenging example I can think of—and it is from my own distant past stage experience—is Seyton in *Macbeth*, who must come on stage after a long absence and say to the Scottish king, "The queen, my lord, is dead." Is he reporting to the king that his wife is dead? Yes. Must it be much more than that? Absolutely.

What This Means for Your Acting

As in Exercise 7, think of every line of a speech as a *new discovery*, an amazing *unfolding of truth in the moment that you did not know of or plan for before you spoke.* This is especially true if you are re-telling a tale you had a part in and already know; you can make discoveries even in the midst of that, realizing for the first time while you are in the middle of just how horrific—or joyous—

the events you are telling of are. One more thing, though: just don't take this as a license to start pausing all the time!

Item 7: Leave Your Hands *Alone*

I recently saw a production of *Titus Andronicus* in which the role of Aaron the Moor was cast with a small man. No problem there; I have seen many performers small in stature deliver performances that were large of size indeed. What was unfortunate was in the costuming Aaron had been saddled with—a cloak that had long sleeves necessary to hold up from sliding down over his hands. In movement this forced the actor, perhaps feeling that he had to try to keep the cuffs from drooping, into constantly bending his elbows with his open palms *upward*. For me this caused the evil Moor to lose all of his power, defiance, and strength. Humor me on this one. The open, palm-up posture, when done constantly, caused the actor to stoop a lot and at best made Aaron into a conniving trickster behind the scenes; perhaps malevolent, but *not* the evil, albeit beautiful specimen of a man who has charmed and illicitly impregnated Tamora, Queen of the Goths. "Palms up" presents to us a physicality that is a *begging, explaining* kind of energy; it is not as strong as simply standing with hands at one's sides, as if to say, "Go ahead; give me your best shot. I can take it and still cut your throat." It is not as strong as Paul Robeson's Othello pronouncing, "I must be *found* . . ."

What This Means for Your Acting

To help with playing strength, the simplest gesture is best. It used to be said that the strongest "acting" position is up straight, feet shoulder-width apart, hands at sides. This places you in a stance in which you are free and able to do whatever the character is required to do—whether classical or contemporary play. Your hands are free to gesture and your legs are free to help you move about the stage with power. Young actors, please take note: the strongest possible posture always begins with hands resting at your sides; I have to confess that unless it helps a character to be defined I would just as soon an actor never cross their hands behind their backs. Without character context and specificity, it just looks like the performer plain doesn't know what do with their hands! The best choice is to leave them alone and let them dangle—and I do mean dangle; don't get all stiff out of nervousness and suddenly lock them into a "robot position." Leave them—and yourself—alone. Allow your shoulders to be relaxed and loose, your hands comfortably at your sides . . . Waiting for you to use them, *only* when you *need* to strike.

Item 8: Speak a Soliloquy as if Your Life Depended upon It—Because It *Does*

A soliloquy is spoken when the character is alone, but it must not be solemn or contemplative, even if the tone of it *is* solemn and contemplative. The greatest soliloquy of all, of course, is "To be, or not to be." Hamlet's thinking out loud is a battle—indeed, think of it as a *battle!*—with the daunting forces we humans must face down here on earth weighed against "The undiscover'd country from whose bourn / No traveller returns." Yes, it is asking questions about whether or not suicide is a way out of a life fraught with sorrow and strife—and by the end of it the answer is a dubious "No." But though the decision by speech's end is to choose life, there is little reassurance. You could believe that the actor might well be exhausted by the end of it because he has been through hell struggling to decide, fighting for an answer to a question that is far out of his reach. This is why soliloquies should be spoken *outside* of you rather than *to* you. Speaking *to* yourself has the pitfall of holding back from the audience, the sense of keeping private when the style of the play demands that you do otherwise. Speaking outside of you is open, forthcoming, presentational, engaging the audience in such a way that causes you to in effect *beg* them for the answer to your problems. The speech can then be active, rather than passive. All Shakespeare must be active, even when a character is just sitting down talking to themselves.

What This Means for Your Acting

When a character is moved to speak out loud about something that is troubling them it is as if they are hanging from a branch over a cliff, begging, shouting, for someone—anyone—to come to their aid and lend a hand. To even open their mouth is a last-ditch effort, a risk that aid will eventually come. Play this scrambling fight when performing a soliloquy, and see what it does to you when the answer does or does not come. No, of course I am not suggesting that you yell, stomp, and foam at the mouth while doing it. I am suggesting that the *need* that drove you to speak it in the first place must push your vocal energy, the desire to be saved—by the *audience*—from that cliff edge is helping you to shape and mold the vowels and consonants as you come pleading to them. Then you will truly be engaging the audience, rather than merely standing in place, talking *at* them.

And by the way: the best focus when speaking a soliloquy is *to the audience*.

Item 9: Pretty Speeches are About Blood and Guts

Near the end of Act II, Scene 1 of *A Midsummer Night's Dream*, Oberon, King of Fairies, speaks a monologue to his dutiful servant Puck. The speech is filled with beautiful imagery— "I know a bank where the wild thyme blows, / Where oxlips and the nodding violet grows, / Quite over-canopied with luscious woodbine, / With sweet musk-roses and with eglantine"—but the actor should avoid getting too precious with the language, too fond of the sound of their own melodic voice. Speeches with lovely images naturally must share those images with the audience, but that is only half of the Shakespearean actor's job. Such speeches come about out of *need driven by love,* either requited or unrequited, and this need must be the driving force that propels the monologue—even if the character is a non-human *fairy*. Before Oberon's pretty speech is over he tells us that he will use the purple flower brought to him by Puck to get even with his unruly wife Titania, seeking to fill her with "hateful fantasies." This speech, like so much of Shakespeare, is multi-layered, is not just about what seems to be on the surface, not just about beauty and not just about love but about so much more, such as *anger at his wife for crossing him.* Finding this will keep the actor from giving in to a "pretty"—but ultimately *boring*—set speech.

What This Means for Your Acting

To play only the beauty of a Shakespeare speech is to play only its mood. It then loses its struggle to get something or overcome something, and is only self-indulgence that does not tell the story of the play and certainly cannot save the character's life. This is where the Bard's ultimate tool, antithesis, will save the day. Even in the midst of a stanza of lovely words, you can—and must—fight for something. Then those words truly can become lovely.

Item 10: *Paint* the Picture!

Because Shakespeare's characters tell the story of the play as they are living the story, they philosophize about every state of their lives; birth, life, beauty, and even as they are at the point of death. The best known of these is Jaques, in his "seven ages of man" speech, where he details every single moment of the aging process even to the moment of death when we are "sans everything." As I have said this great detail is to help the actor build to great heights of despair or joy, but it is more than Shakespeare giving his actors a helping hand at playing emotion.

It is also to sufficiently engage the audience so that the play can, as the Chorus in *Henry V* says, "on your imaginary forces work." In contemporary theatre Shakespeare's script, in a pinch, can be edited for time (audiences of today have shorter attention spans, being busy with so much more to do than Elizabethan audiences did) because he goes into this great detail and then later *repeats* himself again and again, just to make certain his paying customers get it. But that is not the only reason for this; he also did it because Elizabethans *loved it*. Think of yourself around that campfire hearing ghost stories: do you not love to hear every grisly detail, every chilling touch, every gagging moment of the tale, to help you enjoy it better by engaging the mind's eye of your imagination? Here is Claudio, brother to novitiate Isabella in *Measure for Measure*, describing, in more graphic detail than even Hamlet, what it is to die:

> Ay, but to die, and go we know not where;
> To lie in cold obstruction and to rot;
> This sensible warm motion to become
> A kneaded clod; and the delighted spirit
> To bathe in fiery floods, or to reside
> In thrilling region of thick-ribbed ice;
> To be imprison'd in the viewless winds,
> And blown with restless violence round about
> The pendent world; or to be worse than worst
> Of those that lawless and incertain thought
> Imagine howling: 'tis too horrible!
> The weariest and most loathed worldly life
> That age, ache, penury and imprisonment
> Can lay on nature is a paradise
> To what we fear of death.

Though it is gruesome to hear, is it not *delicious* to hear it?

What This Means for Your Acting

Acting Shakespeare you are a storyteller with nothing but his words to tell your story. Truly, in this way, your task is much like radio performers of generations ago, speaking into microphones over vast airwaves with just as much obligation to entertain and move were you in the very room with your listeners. Playwrights of today can skip much of this chore—out of substance as well as style—because we viewers mostly understand their context, but this can cause actors of today to get, well, a little lazy in their performance, occasionally getting too soft at the end of a line or not fully pronouncing a consonant or elongating a vowel. No such indolence is possible with Shakespeare and his words. Use your tongue and lips as brushes, and *paint* the glorious beautiful picture he intended.

Exercise 23: A Pig in Slop—with the Words

I hope you will have fun with this "messy" exercise. It is simple. Perform a monologue—pick one with a long list of images—Mercutio's "Queen Mab" from *Romeo and Juliet*, or Launce's "Crab, my dog" from *The Two Gentlemen of Verona*, or Ford's "Epicurean rascal" speech from *The Merry Wives of Windsor*, perhaps—during which you take on the role of a *pig wallowing in slop*. Yes, that's what I said. You can even fashion an imaginary pigsty on the floor and get down onto all fours and wallow in it, the "slop" being the *words you have to speak*. Have a feast and eat, devour, gobble up in the most disgusting gluttony you can imagine—*feeding* on the *words*. The food you are eating is the words, sounds, consonants, and vowels; you are chewing them, swallowing them, yes even vomiting them out and then repulsively consuming them whole again! *Feast* on the words and images of the Shakespeare monologue by overdoing them, and enjoy that you are doing it! If you are one of those people who are able to belch on cue, do even that! All the while luxuriating in the filthy ecstasy of eating too much. Why do this? To keep reminding yourself that, whether they are glad or whether they are sad, Shakespeare's characters speak *poetry*, make up strange words and rhyme at the end of sentences *on purpose*. You do this same thing today, when life circumstance has caused you to impulsively make up a rhyme or quote aloud a line from a beloved poem or song, because you are suddenly happy or, in grieving reverie, so sad.

The only caution: in doing this exercise just don't let it cause you to mumble or garble or lose energy at the end of a sentence or consonant; the opposite is what you are going after!

What This Means for Your Acting

Sometimes young actors—allowing the pesky "Less is more/I want to do film" dictum creeping into their impressionable minds—gloss over Shakespeare's words. In rehearsal, as you fight to build the most believable performance you are able, you must taste his words with every ounce of spittle you can let fly! Enjoy being a "pig gorging yourself" on the images of Shakespeare. Then, in performance, you will naturally do the speech without the madness while keeping the need to speak because you are driven by an outrageous situation, caused by love.

Item 11: Shakespeare is Too *Big* for Film

I recently saw a pretty fair TV version of *Richard III*. The production acquitted itself well, and I did enjoy it. But I was not in for very long before I realized that what I was seeing was *not* Shakespeare, actually; the cuts to the text were massive—they had to be, certainly—and I was often aware of how the director chose to replace that text with video images and pictures as if to "say" what those glorious, missing words meant (but said better). What I saw was, ultimately, a nice and interesting sticky note of R III, which piqued my interest and my ear sufficiently to go back and read over the full text again. It made me want to see the show on *stage*; the way, of course, it was written to be done in the first place. I then thought of the question of Shakespeare on film, and while there are some fine productions—Kenneth Branagh's *Henry V, Much Ado About Nothing,* and *As You Like It,* Ian McKellen's *Richard III* (adapted from his stage tour I saw years ago at the Brooklyn Academic of Music), Baz Luhrmann's inspired *Romeo + Juliet,* even Al Pacino's worthy *Merchant of Venice*—I felt that the scope and length and breadth of a Shakespeare play (a work, like all theatre, so fueled and propelled by first the spoken word and then our imaginative ears to hear that word) is ultimately too *big* to be captured on celluloid; that film, and all the ways that film can "open up" locations, weather, and even pan up close to see tears of emotion on the actor's cheek, actually *limits and tamps down* the enormous experience of seeing and hearing his work on the "confined" space of a theatrical stage. How ironic that a medium—film—that ostensibly can take the story to its greatest heights actually shrinks down the experience, and through drastic editing of words in favor of (insufficient) pictures to purportedly replace them, robbing the audience of that precious ability to imagine, from the poetry just spoken to them, what all of Shakespeare's stories look like, without being told by a manufactured picture that cannot possibly match the one they are able to draw in their *own minds* . . .

What This Means for Your Acting

First of all what this means is that film is not theatre. What this also means is that, in addition to making the words your own so that you can be believable to an audience, to appear "real" as you play a fairy or a king or a ghost or a man-fish or a woman disguised as a man, you are still on a stage in a room full of people, none of whom is duty bound to genuinely believe that what they are witnessing is real. No amount of everlasting celluloid can take away that personal relationship you have with a live audience, and no one can lesson your obligation to tell them a tale which, through your performance of Shakespeare's words, they can somehow be made to believe *could* be "real."

Item 12: All Shakespearean Characters are *Philosophers* and *Poets*

Even if speaking the most homespun of prose, all of Shakespeare's characters are, in the end, philosophers and poets. Their language is heightened by soaring images, phrases, and made-up words which they both live by in their daily lives as well as employ when necessary for effect. No matter how genuinely you have been able to make sense of the text so that the words become your "own," you are still speaking aloud what is meant to take your listener as well as yourself to a great, lofty place (Nick Bottom after he wakes in *A Midsummer Night's Dream*: "I have had a most rare vision"), so that even the seeming humdrum becomes evidence of a supreme life force greater than yourself. It must also be admitted, as well, that as a Shakespearean character you have indeed been placed in an outrageous situation, and it has been caused by *love*.

What This Means for Your Acting

What this means is that your character is always struggling to find meaning in circumstances that are outrageous, whether those circumstances are dire or delightful. In doing so—and we do this today, not just in the fanciful imaginings of Shakespeare—our words try to climb up to the height of our understanding, to match our outrageous situation. In a sad occasion, upon speaking about someone who has passed on, have you not had the urge—in fact, felt that it was only *appropriate*—that you say *something* to do justice and honor and respect to the memory of your departed friend? These urges are in the hearts of all of Shakespeare's characters in all of his plays, whether a king or a beggar. To again quote from *The Rape of Lucrece*:

> For more it is than I can well express;
> And that deep torture may be called a hell,
> When more is felt than one hath power to tell.

This is how Shakespeare's characters tell the story at the same time that they are living the story; by offering up a philosophical commentary as they express their feelings. Claudio, in the speech above to his sister Isabella, says it all when he proclaims, "'tis too horrible!" when speaking about death. But, in order to make certain that Isabella—as well as the audience—knows just how horrible it is and just how afraid he is of it, his words soar into greater and grizzlier detail. This is similar to the "My Cat is Dead" exercise, because it keeps going on to help the actor rise to the emotion necessary to feel it. All the while—because the audience loved to hear it, remember—the paying customers gobbled it up like the feast for the ear that it also is.

This is what every Shakespearean character is going through, and what we actors of the New Millennium are ever striving to share with our audience.

---

1 The English Sumptuary Law of 1574 (The Statutes of Revels) was enacted so that the very clothing people wore could be regulated so as to maintain the social order of the day. Rich English could donate clothing to licensed theatre companies, such as the Lord Chamberlain's Men and Earl of Leicester's Men, to be worn as costumes in their theatrical productions, thereby avoiding running afoul of the statute by appearing to be too "sumptuous" in their current style of dress. Members of the acting troupes—ostensibly for entertaining theatrical productions—were therefore granted greater latitude in the clothing they wore than the poor of Great Britain, who were prohibited by law from wearing clothing more ornate and grand than their station in society.

POSTSCRIPT

A very ribbon in the cap of youth.

(*Hamlet*)

When I first sat down to prepare these last notes, I considered quoting Prospero's final "Our revels now are ended" speech. But then I realized that it was more about something coming to an end, not a beginning, which is the way I look on your career. At least how I hope it will be this way for you; just getting *started*.

Many years ago I was one of those "voice" actors I have criticized; I thought playing Shakespeare was about sounding grand and melodious, every consonant struck, every vowel legato, everything done so that the audience might get the idea that I was speaking the poetry "beautifully." How wrong I was! Going back to my encounter with the young man who complimented me on my Puck in *Dream*, I eventually learned that the "classical" in classic plays was not going to be found in using a voice that sounded *resonant*; rather it was only going to happen after I had done everything I could to share human need that *resonated* with the *audience*. It became clear to me that no matter what kind of voice an actor has—and I must admit I have a pretty good one—it must be the simple, honest, personal voice you present to an audience when speaking Shakespeare's words. And then, because he has given you the greatest tools an actor could ever imagine, trust in them to carry you and audience alike through the joyous journey that is the experience of William Shakespeare on stage. I also learned that to get there—to find *myself*, you might say—it was indispensable to allow myself to take flight and soar to as many heights as my imagination could take me, through improvisation, exploration, and just plain getting up unafraid of acting a fool, in order to come full circle right back to who I was as a person.

I learned how to be honest by being *outrageous,* and Will Shaksper gave me the words to use to get there.

I hope that I may have helped you get there, too, by getting up on your feet. I hope you have a great time at play—isn't *play* a terrific way to describe this thing we call acting?—and I hope in the process you get acquainted with the actor inside of you bursting to get started, whatever kind of play you are acting in.

As always, good fortune attend your endeavors!

GLOSSARY

A Listing of Common Shakespearean Terminology

If you have been working on Shakespearean text for a while you will probably run into a few words that he uses often. These include words and phrases he contracted to shorten or elide them so they would fit into iambic pentameter rhythm, "nonsense" words he concocted, or archaic idioms found in Elizabethan times. They might seem strange and daunting at first, but the more you read his plays, the more familiar they will become and easier for you to understand. Here is a listing of some of the more common ones (if you can call any of them "common"). For more historical detail about them I recommend the Shakespeare editions published by Folger or Arden, or better yet the New Variorum Shakespeare.

'a: he
abhor: disgust
abuse: deception
addition: title
afeared: afraid
affect: to love
an, and: if
antick: to fool
aroint: get thee gone
ask: to require
attach: to lay hold on

bawcock: a fine fellow
bawd: a pimp (procurer)
beaver: the lower part of a
   helmet
bergomask: a dance
beshrew: evil befall
beteem: to pour out
bodkin: a dagger
bootless: useless
bully-rook: a bragging cheater
by'rlakin: an oath; by our
   little Lady

caitiff: a captive slave
canker: a sore or parasite on a flower
certes: certainly
character: handwriting
cheer: fortune
chuck: a term of endearment
churl: a rude or boorish person
complexion: passion
con: to learn by heart
cony-catch: to cheat
counterfeit: to imitate
cozen: to cheat
cunning: skillful

damask: the color pink
damn: to condemn
dare: to challenge
defy: renounce
despatch or dispatch: to kill or make away with
doff: to strip or put off
done: put to death
dudgeon: a dagger

easy: small or light
envy: spite
eyne: eyes

fadge: to resolve
fain: glad
fardel: a burden
fond: foolish
for: because

forbid: accursed
forfend: to forbid

galliard: a dance
gaudy: festive
gleek: to scoff
good-den: good-evening
government: discretion
gramercy: much thanks

hap: fortune
harry: to annoy or harass
haviour: behavior
honorificabilitudinitatibus: to load with honors. I have included it because I simply could not resist. At 27 letters it is the longest word Shakespeare ever used. It appears in *Love's Labour's Lost,* and is spoken by Costard.
horn-mad: brain-mad
hugger-mugger: secrecy
huswife: a hussy

i'faith: in faith
intentively: attentively
invention: imagination

Jack: a fool
Jack-a-Lent: a puppet
jest: a joke
jovial: pertaining to Jove

Kern: Irish foot soldiers

kickie-wickie: a critical or disrespectful wife
kind: nature
knave: a boy or serving-man
knot: the marriage bond

lay: wager
lewd: foolish
lief: dear
like: to please
lime: to win
livery: a uniform or costume
loon: a low contemptible fellow

made: having one's fortune made
make: to do
mammering: hesitating
match: to join in marriage or to triumph over
mew up: to confine
mickle: much, great
motley: a fool

nephew: grandson
nice: foolish or trivial
ninny: a fool or jester

od's: a contraction of "God's" in exclamations
office: function
ope: to open
or: before

ounce: a tiger
ousel-cock: a blackbird
owe: to own

parlous: shrewd
passionate: to suffer
patch: a mean fellow
pay: to dispatch
point-de-vice: faultless
power: army
prick: to incite
profane: outspoken
proof: strength of manhood

quail: to faint
quake: to cause to tremble
quarrel: a cause
quit: to respond

rash: quick and violent
rate: opinion
respect: consideration
retire: to draw back
rid: to destroy
roundel: a dance or song

sad: serious
safe: to make safe
saucy: lascivious
scan: to examine
scurvy: mean
shame: modesty
shrewd: mischievous
shrive: to confess

sirrah: (pronounced sear-*uh*, not sir-*aah*) a man or boy of inferiority or lower social status
soft: wait a moment
soil: taint
sooth: in truth
sot: fool
speed: fortune
spleen: violent haste
spring: beginning from
square: to quarrel
stale: a prostitute
stilly: softly
stomach: courage
straight: immediately
surcease: to capture by surprise

table: a notebook
tabour: a small drum
take: to infect
tall: strong and valiant
task: challenge
thee: you as the object of a sentence
thine: your
thou: you as the subject of a sentence.
throe: in agony
thrum: weaving thread
thy: your

too too: excessively
toys: foolish tricks
translated: transformed
trow: to trust
true: honest

unhouseled: without receiving the sacrament
unkind: unnatural
use: interest
utter: put forth

vantage: advantage
varlet: a servant
vasty: vast
vaunt: to boast or brag
villain: a low-born man
virtue: valor

wax: to grow
welkin: the sky
wend: to go
wit: wisdom or knowledge
wittol: a cuckold
worship: to honor
wot: to know
wroth: misfortune

yare: to be ready
yaw: out of control
ye: you plural
yield: to reward or report

Appendix

PRACTICE SPEECHES FOR MEN AND WOMEN

Here are a few speeches you can use to work on. You can also of course find your own; the choice is huge. Some are in prose and some in blank verse, so try one of each. As always I urge you to start reading and memorizing right away, to allow yourself to *feel* the memorization coming, as it honestly will, out of repeating the rhythm of the words. Again I have intentionally left out any footnotes or synopses, though I did add the act and scene numbers so that you can learn a bit more after you've taken them out for a spin (I am guessing that even the playwright himself would not object to you having those). In the meantime, act, and ask questions later. Let Shakespeare's *words* tell you what to do . . .

Men

Dramatic Speeches

Romeo and Juliet

CHORUS

Two households, both alike in dignity,
In fair Verona, where we lay our scene,
From ancient grudge break to new mutiny,
Where civil blood makes civil hands unclean.

From forth the fatal loins of these two foes
A pair of star-cross'd lovers take their life;
Whose misadventured piteous overthrows
Do with their death bury their parents' strife.
The fearful passage of their death-mark'd love,
And the continuance of their parents' rage,
Which, but their children's end, nought could remove,
Is now the two hours' traffic of our stage;
The which if you with patient ears attend,
What here shall miss, our toil shall strive to mend.
                                                (Prologue)

MERCUTIO

O, then, I see Queen Mab hath been with you.
She is the fairies' midwife, and she comes
In shape no bigger than an agate-stone
On the fore-finger of an alderman,
Drawn with a team of little atomies
Athwart men's noses as they lie asleep;
Her wagon-spokes made of long spiders' legs,
The cover of the wings of grasshoppers,
The traces of the smallest spider's web,
The collars of the moonshine's watery beams,
Her whip of cricket's bone, the lash of film,
Her wagoner a small grey-coated gnat,
Not so big as a round little worm
Prick'd from the lazy finger of a maid;
Her chariot is an empty hazel-nut
Made by the joiner squirrel or old grub,
Time out o' mind the fairies' coachmakers.
And in this state she gallops night by night
Through lovers' brains, and then they dream of love;
O'er courtiers' knees, that dream on court'sies straight,
O'er lawyers' fingers, who straight dream on fees,
O'er ladies' lips, who straight on kisses dream,

Which oft the angry Mab with blisters plagues,
Because their breaths with sweetmeats tainted are:
Sometime she gallops o'er a courtier's nose,
And then dreams he of smelling out a suit;
And sometime comes she with a tithe-pig's tail
Tickling a parson's nose as a' lies asleep,
Then dreams, he of another benefice:
Sometime she driveth o'er a soldier's neck,
And then dreams he of cutting foreign throats,
Of breaches, ambuscadoes, Spanish blades,
Of healths five-fathom deep; and then anon
Drums in his ear, at which he starts and wakes,
And being thus frighted swears a prayer or two
And sleeps again. This is that very Mab
That plats the manes of horses in the night,
And bakes the elflocks in foul sluttish hairs,
Which once untangled, much misfortune bodes:
This is the hag, when maids lie on their backs,
That presses them and learns them first to bear,
Making them women of good carriage:
This is she—

(Act I, Scene 4)

ROMEO

But, soft! what light through yonder window breaks?
It is the east, and Juliet is the sun.
Arise, fair sun, and kill the envious moon,
Who is already sick and pale with grief,
That thou her maid art far more fair than she:
Be not her maid, since she is envious;
Her vestal livery is but sick and green
And none but fools do wear it; cast it off.
It is my lady, O, it is my love!
O, that she knew she were!
She speaks yet she says nothing: what of that?

Her eye discourses; I will answer it.
I am too bold, 'tis not to me she speaks:
Two of the fairest stars in all the heaven,
Having some business, do entreat her eyes
To twinkle in their spheres till they return.
What if her eyes were there, they in her head?
The brightness of her cheek would shame those stars,
As daylight doth a lamp; her eyes in heaven
Would through the airy region stream so bright
That birds would sing and think it were not night.
See, how she leans her cheek upon her hand!
O, that I were a glove upon that hand,
That I might touch that cheek!
                            (Act II, Scene 2)

Hamlet

CLAUDIUS

O, my offence is rank it smells to heaven;
It hath the primal eldest curse upon't,
A brother's murder. Pray can I not,
Though inclination be as sharp as will:
My stronger guilt defeats my strong intent;
And, like a man to double business bound,
I stand in pause where I shall first begin,
And both neglect. What if this cursed hand
Were thicker than itself with brother's blood,
Is there not rain enough in the sweet heavens
To wash it white as snow? Whereto serves mercy
But to confront the visage of offence?
And what's in prayer but this two-fold force,
To be forestall'd ere we come to fall,
Or pardon'd being down? Then I'll look up;
My fault is past. But, O, what form of prayer
Can serve my turn? "Forgive me my foul murder"?

That cannot be; since I am still possess'd
Of those effects for which I did the murder,
My crown, mine own ambition and my queen.
May one be pardon'd and retain the offence?
In the corrupted currents of this world
Offence's gilded hand may shove by justice,
And oft 'tis seen the wicked prize itself
Buys out the law: but 'tis not so above;
There is no shuffling, there the action lies
In his true nature; and we ourselves compell'd,
Even to the teeth and forehead of our faults,
To give in evidence. What then? what rests?
Try what repentance can: what can it not?
Yet what can it when one cannot repent?
O wretched state! O bosom black as death!
O limed soul, that, struggling to be free,
Art more engaged! Help, angels! Make assay!
Bow, stubborn knees; and, heart with strings of steel,
Be soft as sinews of the newborn babe!
All may be well.

(Act III, Scene 3)

Comedic Speeches

A Midsummer Night's Dream

BOTTOM

[Awaking] When my cue comes, call me, and I will answer: my next is, "Most fair Pyramus." Heigh-ho! Peter Quince! Flute, the bellows-mender! Snout, the tinker! Starveling! God's my life, stolen hence, and left me asleep! I have had a most rare vision. I have had a dream, past the wit of man to say what dream it was: man is but an ass, if he go about to expound this dream. Methought I was—there is no man can tell what. Methought I was,—and methought

I had,—but man is but a patched fool, if he will offer to
say what methought I had. The eye of man hath not
heard, the ear of man hath not seen, man's hand is not
able to taste, his tongue to conceive, nor his heart to
report, what my dream was. I will get Peter Quince to
write a ballad of this dream: it shall be called Bottom's
Dream, because it hath no bottom; and I will sing it in the
latter end of a play, before the duke: peradventure, to
make it the more gracious, I shall sing it at her death.
(Act IV, Scene 1)

The Merry Wives of Windsor

FORD

What a damned Epicurean rascal is this! My heart is ready
to crack with impatience. Who says this is improvident
jealousy? my wife hath sent to him; the hour is fixed; the
match is made. Would any man have thought this? See the
hell of having a false woman! My bed shall be abused, my
coffers ransacked, my reputation gnawn at; and I shall not
only receive this villainous wrong, but stand under the
adoption of abominable terms, and by him that does me
this wrong. Terms! Names! Amaimon sounds well; Lucifer,
well; Barbason, well; yet they are devils' additions, the
names of fiends: but Cuckold! Wittol!—Cuckold! The devil
himself hath not such a name. Page is an ass, a secure ass:
he will trust his wife; he will not be jealous. I will rather
trust a Fleming with my butter, Parson Hugh the
Welshman with my cheese, an Irishman with my aqua-vitae
bottle, or a thief to walk my ambling gelding, than my wife
with herself; then she plots, then she ruminates, then she
devises; and what they think in their hearts they may
effect, they will break their hearts but they will effect. God
be praised for my jealousy! Eleven o'clock the hour. I will
prevent this, detect my wife, be revenged on Falstaff, and

laugh at Page. I will about it; better three hours too soon than a minute too late. Fie, fie, fie! Cuckold! Cuckold! Cuckold!

(Act II, Scene 2)

FALSTAFF

Go fetch me a quart of sack; put a toast in't. Have I lived to be carried in a basket, like a barrow of butcher's offal, and to be thrown in the Thames? Well, if I be served such another trick, I'll have my brains ta'en out and buttered, and give them to a dog for a new-year's gift. The rogues slighted me into the river with as little remorse as they would have drowned a blind bitch's puppies, fifteen i' the litter: and you may know by my size that I have a kind of alacrity in sinking; if the bottom were as deep as hell, I should down. I had been drowned, but that the shore was shelvy and shallow,—a death that I abhor; for the water swells a man; and what a thing should I have been when I had been swelled! I should have been a mountain of mummy.

(Act III, Scene 5)

FALSTAFF

Nay, you shall hear, Master Brook, what I have suffered to bring this woman to evil for your good. Being thus crammed in the basket, a couple of Ford's knaves, his hinds, were called forth by their mistress to carry me in the name of foul clothes to Datchet-lane: they took me on their shoulders; met the jealous knave their master in the door, who asked them once or twice what they had in their basket: I quaked for fear, lest the lunatic knave would have searched it; but fate, ordaining he should be a cuckold, held his hand. Well: on went he for a search, and away went I for foul clothes. But mark the sequel, Master

Brook: I suffered the pangs of three several deaths; first, an intolerable fright, to be detected with a jealous rotten bell-wether; next, to be compassed, like a good bilbo, in the circumference of a peck, hilt to point, heel to head; and then, to be stopped in, like a strong distillation, with stinking clothes that fretted in their own grease: think of that,—a man of my kidney,—think of that,—that am as subject to heat as butter; a man of continual dissolution and thaw: it was a miracle to scape suffocation. And in the height of this bath, when I was more than half stewed in grease, like a Dutch dish, to be thrown into the Thames, and cooled, glowing hot, in that surge, like a horse-shoe; think of that,—hissing hot,—think of that, Master Brook.

(Act III, Scene 5)

The Two Gentlemen of Verona

LAUNCE

Nay, 'twill be this hour ere I have done weeping; all the kind of the Launces have this very fault. I have received my proportion, like the prodigious son, and am going with Sir Proteus to the Imperial's court. I think Crab, my dog, be the sourest-natured dog that lives: my mother weeping, my father wailing, my sister crying, our maid howling, our cat wringing her hands, and all our house in a great perplexity, yet did not this cruel-hearted cur shed one tear: he is a stone, a very pebble stone, and has no more pity in him than a dog: a Jew would have wept to have seen our parting; why, my grandam, having no eyes, look you, wept herself blind at my parting. Nay, I'll show you the manner of it. This shoe is my father: no, this left shoe is my father: no, no, this left shoe is my mother: nay, that cannot be so neither: yes, it is so, it is so, it hath the worser sole. This shoe, with the hole in it, is my mother, and this my father; a vengeance on't! there 'tis: now, sit, this staff is my sister, for, look you, she is as white as a lily and as small as a wand: this hat is Nan, our maid: I am the dog: no, the dog is himself, and I am the dog—Oh! the dog is me, and I am myself; ay, so, so. Now come I to my father; Father, your blessing: now should not the shoe speak a word for weeping: now should I kiss my father; well, he weeps on. Now come I to my mother: O, that she could speak now like a wood woman! Well, I kiss her; why, there 'tis; here's my mother's breath up and down. Now come I to my sister; mark the moan she makes. Now the dog all this while sheds not a tear nor speaks a word; but see how I lay the dust with my tears.

(Act II, Scene 3)

Much Ado About Nothing

BENEDICK

I do much wonder that one man, seeing how much another man is a fool when he dedicates his behaviors to love, will, after he hath laughed at such shallow follies in others, become the argument of his own scorn by failing in love: and such a man is Claudio. I have known when there was no music with him but the drum and the fife; and now had he rather hear the tabour and the pipe: I have known when he would have walked ten mile a-foot to see a good armour; and now will he lie ten nights awake, carving the fashion of a new doublet. He was wont to speak plain and to the purpose, like an honest man and a soldier; and now is he turned orthography; his words are a very fantastical banquet, just so many strange dishes. May I be so converted and see with these eyes? I cannot tell; I think not: I will not be sworn, but love may transform me to an oyster; but I'll take my oath on it, till he have made an oyster of me, he shall never make me such a fool. One woman is fair, yet I am well; another is wise, yet I am well; another virtuous, yet I am well; but till all graces be in one woman, one woman shall not come in my grace. Rich she shall be, that's certain; wise, or I'll none; virtuous, or I'll never cheapen her; fair, or I'll never look on her; mild, or come not near me; noble, or not I for an angel; of good discourse, an excellent musician, and her hair shall be of what colour it please God.

(Act II, Scene 3)

BENEDICK

This can be no trick. The conference was sadly borne. They have the truth of this from Hero. They seem to pity the lady. It seems her affections have their full bent. Love me? Why, it must be requited. I hear how I am censured. They say I will bear myself proudly if I perceive the love come from her. They say too that she will rather die than give any sign of affection. I did never think to marry. I must not seem proud. Happy are they that hear their detractions and can put them to mending. They say the lady is fair. 'Tis a truth, I can bear them witness. And virtuous—'tis so, I cannot reprove it. And wise, but for loving me. By my troth, it is no addition to her wit—nor no great argument of her folly, for I will be horribly in love with her. I may chance have some odd quirks and remnants of wit broken on me because I have railed so long against marriage; but doth not the appetite alter? A man loves the meat in his youth that he cannot endure in his age. Shall quips and sentences and these paper bullets of the brain awe a man from the career of his humor? No. The world must be peopled. When I said I would die a bachelor, I did not think I should live till I were married. Here comes Beatrice. By this day, she's a fair lady! I do spy some marks of love in her.

(Act II, Scene 3)

Women

Dramatic Speeches

Romeo and Juliet

JULIET

The clock struck nine when I did send the nurse;
In half an hour she promised to return.
Perchance she cannot meet him: that's not so.
O, she is lame! love's heralds should be thoughts,
Which ten times faster glide than the sun's beams,
Driving back shadows over louring hills:
Therefore do nimble-pinion'd doves draw love,
And therefore hath the wind-swift Cupid wings.
Now is the sun upon the highmost hill
Of this day's journey, and from nine till twelve
Is three long hours, yet she is not come.
Had she affections and warm youthful blood,
She would be as swift in motion as a ball;
My words would bandy her to my sweet love,
And his to me:
But old folks, many feign as they were dead;
Unwieldy, slow, heavy and pale as lead.
O God, she comes!
                              (Act II, Scene 5)

JULIET

Gallop apace, you fiery-footed steeds,
Towards Phoebus' lodging: such a wagoner
As Phaethon would whip you to the west,
And bring in cloudy night immediately.
Spread thy close curtain, love-performing night,
That runaway's eyes may wink and Romeo

Leap to these arms, untalk'd of and unseen.
Lovers can see to do their amorous rites
By their own beauties; or, if love be blind,
It best agrees with night. Come, civil night,
Thou sober-suited matron, all in black,
And learn me how to lose a winning match,
Play'd for a pair of stainless maidenhoods:
Hood my unmann'd blood, bating in my cheeks,
With thy black mantle; till strange love, grown bold,
Think true love acted simple modesty.
Come, night; come, Romeo; come, thou day in night;
For thou wilt lie upon the wings of night
Whiter than new snow on a raven's back.
Come, gentle night, come, loving, black-brow'd night,
Give me my Romeo; and, when he shall die,
Take him and cut him out in little stars,
And he will make the face of heaven so fine
That all the world will be in love with night
And pay no worship to the garish sun.
O, I have bought the mansion of a love,
But not possess'd it, and, though I am sold,
Not yet enjoy'd: so tedious is this day
As is the night before some festival
To an impatient child that hath new robes
And may not wear them. O, here comes my nurse,
And she brings news; and every tongue that speaks
But Romeo's name speaks heavenly eloquence.

(Act III, Scene 2)

Henry VI, Part 1

JOAN

Dauphin, I am by birth a shepherd's daughter,
My wit untrained in any kind of art.
Heaven and our Lady gracious hath it pleased

To shine on my contemptible estate.
Lo, whilst I waited on my tender lambs,
And to sun's parching heat displayed my cheeks,
God's mother deigned to appear to me,
And in a vision, full of majesty,
Willed me to leave my base vocation
And free my country from calamity.
Her aid she promised, and assured success.
In complete glory she revealed herself—
And whereas I was black and swart before,
With those clear rays which she infused on me
That beauty am I blest with, which you may see.
Ask me what question thou canst possible,
And I will answer unpremeditated.
My courage try by combat, if thou dar'st,
And thou shalt find that I exceed my sex.
Resolve on this: thou shalt be fortunate,
If thou receive me for thy warlike mate.
                              (Act I, Scene 3)

Henry IV, Part 1

LADY PERCY

O, my good lord, why are you thus alone?
For what offence have I this fortnight been
A banished woman from my Harry's bed?
Tell me, sweet lord, what is't that takes from thee
Thy stomach, pleasure and thy golden sleep?
Why dost thou bend thine eyes upon the earth,
And start so often when thou sit'st alone?
Why hast thou lost the fresh blood in thy cheeks
And given my treasures and my rights of thee
To thick-eyed musing and cursed melancholy?
In thy faint slumbers I by thee have watched,
And heard thee murmur tales of iron wars,

Speak terms of manage to thy bounding steed,
Cry "Courage! to the field!" And thou hast talked
Of sallies and retires, of trenches, tents,
Of palisadoes, frontiers, parapets,
Of basilisks, of cannon, culverin,
Of prisoners' ransom and of soldiers slain,
And all the currents of a heady fight.
Thy spirit within thee hath been so at war,
And thus hath so bestirred thee in thy sleep,
That beads of sweat have stood upon thy brow
Like bubbles in a late-disturbed stream,
And in thy face strange motions have appeared,
Such as we see when men restrain their breath
On some great sudden hest. O, what portents are these?
Some heavy business hath my lord in hand,
And I must know it, else he loves me not.
                                        (Act II, Scene 3)

Measure for Measure

ISABELLA

To whom should I complain? Did I tell this,
Who would believe me? O perilous mouths,
That bear in them one and the self-same tongue,
Either of condemnation or approof;
Bidding the law make court'sy to their will:
Hooking both right and wrong to the appetite,
To follow as it draws! I'll to my brother:
Though he hath fallen by promputre of the blood,
Yet hath he in him such a mind of honour.
That, had he twenty heads to tender down
On twenty bloody blocks, he'd yield them up,
Before his sister should her body stoop
To such abhorr'd pollution.
Then, Isabel, live chaste, and, brother, die:

More than our brother is our chastity.
I'll tell him yet of Angelo's request,
And fit his mind to death, for his soul's rest.
(Act II, Scene 4)

All's Well That Ends Well

HELENA

Then, I confess,
Here on my knee, before high heaven and you,
That before you, and next unto high heaven,
I love your son.
My friends were poor, but honest; so's my love:
Be not offended; for it hurts not him
That he is loved of me: I follow him not
By any token of presumptuous suit;
Nor would I have him till I do deserve him;
Yet never know how that desert should be.
I know I love in vain, strive against hope;
Yet in this captious and intenible sieve
I still pour in the waters of my love
And lack not to lose still: thus, Indian-like,
Religious in mine error, I adore
The sun, that looks upon his worshipper,
But knows of him no more. My dearest madam,
Let not your hate encounter with my love
For loving where you do: but if yourself,
Whose aged honour cites a virtuous youth,
Did ever in so true a flame of liking
Wish chastely and love dearly, that your Dian
Was both herself and love: O, then, give pity
To her, whose state is such that cannot choose
But lend and give where she is sure to lose;
That seeks not to find that her search implies,
But riddle-like lives sweetly where she dies!
(Act I, Scene 3)

APPENDIX: PRACTICE SPEECHES

The Winter's Tale

PAULINA

What studied torments, tyrant, hast for me?
What wheels? racks? fires? what flaying? boiling?
In leads or oils? What old or newer torture
Must I receive, whose every word deserves
To taste of thy most worst? Thy tyranny,
Together working with thy jealousies
(Fancies too weak for boys, too green and idle
For girls of nine), O think what they have done
And then run mad indeed: stark mad! For all
Thy by-gone fooleries were but spices of it.
That thou betray'dst Polixenes, 'twas nothing;
That did but show thee, of a fool, inconstant
And damnable ingrateful: nor was't much,
Thou wouldst have poison'd good Camillo's honour,
To have him kill a king; poor trespasses,
More monstrous standing by: whereof I reckon
The casting forth to crows thy baby daughter,
To be or none or little; though a devil
Would have shed water out of fire ere done't:
Nor is't directly laid to thee, the death
Of the young prince, whose honourable thoughts
(Thoughts high for one so tender) cleft the heart
That could conceive a gross and foolish sire
Blemish'd his gracious dam: this is not, no,
Laid to thy answer: but the last—O lords,
When I have said, cry "woe!"—the queen, the queen,
The sweet'st, dear'st creature's dead: and vengeance for't
Not dropp'd down yet.

(Act III, Scene 2)

Comedic Speeches

The Comedy of Errors

ADRIANA

Ay, ay, Antipholus, look strange and frown:
Some other mistress hath thy sweet aspects;
I am not Adriana nor thy wife.
The time was once when thou unurged wouldst vow
That never words were music to thine ear,
That never object pleasing in thine eye,
That never touch well welcome to thy hand,
That never meat sweet-savor'd in thy taste,
Unless I spake, or look'd, or touch'd, or carved to thee.
How comes it now, my husband, O, how comes it,
That thou art thus estranged from thyself?
Thyself I call it, being strange to me,
That, undividable, incorporate,
Am better than thy dear self's better part.
Ah, do not tear away thyself from me!
For know, my love, as easy mayest thou fall
A drop of water in the breaking gulf,
And take unmingled that same drop again,
Without addition or diminishing,
As take from me thyself and not me too.
How dearly would it touch me to the quick,
Shouldst thou but hear I were licentious
And that this body, consecrate to thee,
By ruffian lust should be contaminate!
Wouldst thou not spit at me and spurn at me
And hurl the name of husband in my face
And tear the stain'd skin off my harlot-brow
And from my false hand cut the wedding-ring
And break it with a deep-divorcing vow?
I know thou canst; and therefore see thou do it.

I am possess'd with an adulterate blot;
My blood is mingled with the crime of lust:
For if we too be one and thou play false,
I do digest the poison of thy flesh,
Being strumpeted by thy contagion.
Keep then far league and truce with thy true bed;
I live unstain'd, thou undishonoured.

(Act I, Scene 4)

The Tempest

MIRANDA

I do not know
One of my sex; no woman's face remember,
Save, from my glass, mine own; nor have I seen
More that I may call men than you, good friend,
And my dear father: how features are abroad,
I am skilless of; but, by my modesty,
The jewel in my dower, I would not wish
Any companion in the world but you,
Nor can imagination form a shape,
Besides yourself, to like of. But I prattle
Something too wildly and my father's precepts
I therein do forget.

(Act III, Scene 1)

The Taming of the Shrew

KATHERINA

The more my wrong, the more his spite appears:
What, did he marry me to famish me?
Beggars, that come unto my father's door,
Upon entreaty have a present aims;

If not, elsewhere they meet with charity:
But I, who never knew how to entreat,
Nor never needed that I should entreat,
Am starved for meat, giddy for lack of sleep,
With oath kept waking and with brawling fed:
And that which spites me more than all these wants,
He does it under name of perfect love;
As who should say, if I should sleep or eat,
'Twere deadly sickness or else present death.
I prithee go and get me some repast;
I care not what, so it be wholesome food.

(Act IV, Scene 3)

A Midsummer Night's Dream

HELENA

How happy some o'er other some can be!
Through Athens I am thought as fair as she.
But what of that? Demetrius thinks not so;
He will not know what all but he do know:
And as he errs, doting on Hermia's eyes,
So I, admiring of his qualities:
Things base and vile, folding no quantity,
Love can transpose to form and dignity:
Love looks not with the eyes, but with the mind;
And therefore is wing'd Cupid painted blind:
Nor hath Love's mind of any judgement taste;
Wings and no eyes figure unheedy haste:
And therefore is Love said to be a child,
Because in choice he is so oft beguiled.
As waggish boys in game themselves forswear,
So the boy Love is perjured everywhere:
For ere Demetrius look'd on Hermia's eyne,
He hail'd down oaths that he was only mine;
And when this hail some heat from Hermia felt,

So he dissolved, and showers of oaths did melt.
I will go tell him of fair Hermia's flight:
Then to the wood will he to-morrow night
Pursue her; and for this intelligence
If I have thanks, it is a dear expense:
But herein mean I to enrich my pain,
To have his sight thither and back again.

(Act I, Scene 1)

Two Gentlemen of Verona

JULIA

This babble shall not henceforth trouble me.
Here is a coil with protestation! (*Tears the letter*)
O hateful hands, to tear such loving words!
Injurious wasps, to feed on such sweet honey
And kill the bees that yield it with your stings!
I'll kiss each several paper for amends.
Look, here is writ "kind Julia": unkind Julia!
As in revenge of thy ingratitude,
I throw thy name against the bruising stones,
Trampling contemptuously on thy disdain.
And here is writ "love wounded Proteus":
Poor wounded name! My bosom, as a bed
Shall lodge thee till thy wound be thoroughly heal'd;
And thus I search it with a sovereign kiss.
But twice or thrice was "Proteus" written down:
Be calm, good wind, blow not a word away
Till I have found each letter in the letter
Except mine own name; that some whirlwind bear
Unto a ragged, fearful-hanging rock,
And throw it thence into the raging sea!
Lo! Here in one line is his name twice writ,
"Poor forlorn Proteus, passionate Proteus,
To the sweet Julia": that I'll tear away;

And yet I will not, sith so prettily
He couples it to his complaining names:
Thus will I fold them one upon another:
Now kiss, embrace, contend, do what you will.
(Act I, Scene 2)

As You Like It

ROSALIND

And why, I pray you? Who might be your mother,
That you insult, exult, and all at once,
Over the wretched? What though you have no beauty,—
As, by my faith, I see no more in you
Than without candle may go dark to bed—
Must you be therefore proud and pitiless?
Why, what means this? Why do you look on me?
I see no more in you than in the ordinary
Of nature's sale-work. 'Od's my little life,
I think she means to tangle my eyes too!
No, faith, proud mistress, hope not after it:
'Tis not your inky brows, your black silk hair,
Your bugle eyeballs, nor your cheek of cream,
That can entame my spirits to your worship.
You foolish shepherd, wherefore do you follow her,
Like foggy south puffing with wind and rain?
You are a thousand times a properer man
Than she a woman: 'tis such fools as you
That makes the world full of ill-favour'd children:
'Tis not her glass, but you, that flatters her;
And out of you she sees herself more proper
Than any of her lineaments can show her.
But, mistress, know yourself: down on your knees,
And thank heaven, fasting, for a good man's love:
For I must tell you friendly in your ear,
Sell when you can: you are not for all markets:

Cry the man mercy; love him; take his offer:
Foul is most foul, being foul to be a scoffer.
So take her to thee, shepherd: fare you well.
(Act III, Scene 5)

ROSALIND

It is not the fashion to see the lady the epilogue;
but it is no more unhandsome than to see the lord
the prologue. If it be true that good wine needs
no bush, 'tis true that a good play needs no
epilogue; yet to good wine they do use good bushes,
and good plays prove the better by the help of good
epilogues. What a case am I in then, that am
neither a good epilogue nor cannot insinuate with
you in the behalf of a good play! I am not
furnished like a beggar, therefore to beg will not
become me: my way is to conjure you; and I'll begin
with the women. I charge you, O women, for the love
you bear to men, to like as much of this play as
please you: and I charge you, O men, for the love
you bear to women—as I perceive by your simpering,
none of you hates them—that between you and the
women the play may please. If I were a woman I
would kiss as many of you as had beards that pleased
me, complexions that liked me and breaths that I
defied not: and, I am sure, as many as have good
beards or good faces or sweet breaths will, for my
kind offer, when I make curtsy, bid me farewell.
(Act V, Scene 4)

PHEBE

Think not I love him, though I ask for him:
'Tis but a peevish boy; yet he talks well;
But what care I for words? yet words do well

When he that speaks them pleases those that hear.
It is a pretty youth: not very pretty:
But, sure, he's proud, and yet his pride becomes him:
He'll make a proper man: the best thing in him
Is his complexion; and faster than his tongue
Did make offence his eye did heal it up.
He is not very tall; yet for his years he's tall:
His leg is but so so; and yet 'tis well:
There was a pretty redness in his lip,
A little riper and more lusty red
Than that mix'd in his cheek; 'twas just the difference
Between the constant red and mingled damask.
There be some women, Silvius, had they mark'd him
In parcels as I did, would have gone near
To fall in love with him; but, for my part,
I love him not nor hate him not; and yet
I have more cause to hate him than to love him:
For what had he to do to chide at me?
He said mine eyes were black and my hair black:
And, now I am remember'd, scorn'd at me:
I marvel why I answer'd not again:
But that's all one; omittance is no quittance.
I'll write to him a very taunting letter,
And thou shalt bear it: wilt thou, Silvius?

(Act III, Scene 5)

RECOMMENDED READING

Acting in Shakespeare, by Robert Cohen (Smith and Kraus, 2005)
The Arden Dictionary of Shakespeare Quotations, compiled by Jane Armstrong (Arden Shakespeare, 1999)
The Arden Shakespeare Complete Works, edited by Richard Proudpoot, Ann Thompson, and David Scott Kastan (Thomas Nelson Publishers, 1998)
A Practical Handbook for the Actor, by Melissa Bruder, Lee Michael Cohen, Madeleine Olnek, and Scott Zigler (Vintage Books, 1986)
The Shakespeare Book of Lists, by Michael Lomoncico (New Page Books, 2001)
Shakespeare for Beginners, by Brandon Toropov (Writers and Readers Publishing, 1997, 1999)
The Shakespeare Miscellany, by David Crystal and Ben Crystal (The Overlook Press, 2005)
Shakespeare on Toast, by Ben Crystal (Icon Books, 2009)
The Stanislavski System: The Professional Training of an Actor; Second Revised Edition, by Sonia Moore (Penguin Handbooks, 1984)
A Year in the Life of William Shakespeare, by James Shapiro (HarperCollins, 2005)

Websites

www.playshakespeare.com/
www.histm/news/history-lists/10-things-ory.coyou-didnt-know-about-william-shakespeare
http://absoluteshakespeare.com/
www.bardweb.net/content/ac/sources.html
www.shakespeare-online.com/biography/shakespeare name.html
www.shakespeareswords.com/
www.literarydevices.com/couplet/
whatsitallaboutshakespeare.blogspot.com/2012/03/what-are-shakespeares-problem-plays.html

INDEX

acting/actors: boy players 23–4; cold reading 60–2, 93, 96–7, 110; cue acting 24–5; in Elizabethan time 21–3; pausing 119–20, 168; picking up one's cues 120; picking up one's cues and shared lines 125; thrust stage acting 16, 31–2, 158, 159; "voice" actors 178; warm-up 63–6; women's roles played by boys/men 15–16, 23–4; *see also* doing Shakespeare; film work; lessons; practice speeches (men); practice speeches (women); Shakespeare's poetry
African American Baptist church tradition 101–2
agape 7
alexandrines 129
All's Well That Ends Well: Boccaccio's *The Decameron* as source 57; practice speech (women) 198; "problem play" 34, 40; synopsis 40
amphibrachs 121
anapests 121, 128
antithesis: concept 94, 164–5; "play the antithesis" exercise 165–7; and "pretty" speeches 171
Antony and Cleopatra: Plutarch as source 56; synopsis 51
The Arden Shakespeare 180
As You Like It: Celia's and Rosalind's "Herein I see thou lov'st me not" scene 115–16; Duke Frederick's and Oliver's "Not see him since?" scene 113–14; Jaques' and Touchtone's use of prose 146; Jaques' "seven ages of man" speech 171; Kenneth Branagh's film 175; Oliver's and Orlando's "Now, sir! what make you here?" scene 111–13; Orlando's "Hang there, my verse" speech 79, 83; Orlando's "O good old man" speech 114; Phebe and Silvius

(Act III, Scene 5) 116–17, 146, 205–6; *philia* in 7; plot twists and boy players 23; practice speeches (women) 204–6; Rosalind and Phebe (Act III, Scene 5) 113, 204–6; synopsis 38–9; use of poetry and prose 118
audience: in Elizabethan time 16, 19–21; speaking directly to 32

Bacon, Francis 14
Baptist church tradition 101–2
Barton, John, *Playing Shakespeare* 88
bear-baiting 20, 156
Beckett, Samuel, *Waiting for Godot* 33
"become the words" exercise 76–9
big and loud, "size is more than big and loud" 159–61
Blackfriars Theatre (London) 159
blank verse (verse without rhyme) 90, 118, 119–20, 145, 147; *see also* iambic pentameters; "verse" lesson
blood and guts, "pretty speeches are about blood and guts" 170–1
Boas, Frederick Samuel 34, 40
Boccaccio, Giovanni, *The Decameron* 57
book overview 10–11
boy players 23–4

Branagh, Kenneth, Shakespeare films 147, 175
Brooke, Arthur, *The Tragical History of Romeus and Juliet* 57
Buchell, Arend van (Arnoldus Buchelius) 17
Burbage, Richard 22, 61

caesuras 120, 129
candle lighting 19
capping couplets 127, 133, 142
Cardenio (with John Fletcher) 57
caritas 7
Caxton, William 25
characters, "all Shakespearean characters are *philosophers* and *poets*" 176–7
charades (game) 76, 79
Chaucer, Geoffrey, *Knight's Tale* 56
Chekhov, Anton 155
choruses, and use of rhyme verse 131
Chronicles of England, Scotland and Ireland (Raphael Holinshed) 57
cock-fighting 20
cold reading 60–2, 93, 96–7, 110
Coleridge, Samuel Taylor 32; *see also* "willing suspension of disbelief"
comedies, white flag atop theater 18
comedies (synopses): *All's Well That Ends Well* 40; *As You Like*

It 38–9; *The Comedy of Errors* 34; *Love's Labour's Lost* 36; *Measure for Measure* 40–1; *The Merchant of Venice* 37; *The Merry Wives of Windsor* 39; *A Midsummer Night's Dream* 36–7; *Much Ado About Nothing* 37–8; *The Taming of the Shrew* 35; *Troilus and Cressida* 39–40; *Twelfth Night* 38; *The Two Gentlemen of Verona* 35–6

The Comedy of Errors: Dromio's "Return'd so soon!" speech 70; practice speech (women) 200–1; prose for low comedy scene 146; synopsis 34

Condell, Henry 15

consonants, actors' best friends 66, 88, 89

Cooke, Alexander 24

copyright 25

Coriolanus: Plutarch as source 56; synopsis 51–2

couplets: about 132–3; capping couplets 127, 133, 142; couplets between two characters 133–41

cue acting 24–5

cue scripting 25

cue scripts 22, 25–6, 30–1; *A Midsummer Night's Dream* examples 26–30

Cymbeline: Boccaccio's *The Decameron* as source 57; plot twists and boy players 23; synopsis 54–5

dactyls 121, 129

dancing, followed by speaking 73–4

Dench, Judi 147

de Vere, Edward, 17th Earl of Oxford 15

diction 65–6

discovery, "don't report, make a discovery!" 167–8

"discovery place" 16

"divers schedules" passage (*Twelfth Night*) 153

doing *see* "doing" lesson; doing Shakespeare; "play what the scene is *doing*"

"doing" lesson: become the words 76–9; don't think about it 69–71; every line is a new discovery 75–6; hop, kneel, crawl, and hug! 72–3; howl 66–8; sing 68–9; wrestle, kick, speak! 73–4; you are being chased 74–5

doing Shakespeare: acting Shakespeare vs. "Shakespearean" acting 57–9; "all Shakespearean characters are *philosophers* and *poets*" 176–7; antithesis and "play the antithesis" exercise 164–7; "don't report, make a discovery!" 167–8; "leave your hands *alone*" 168–9; "*paint* the picture" and "A Pig in Slop" exercise 171–4; "play what the scene is *doing*" 161–4; "pretty speeches are

about blood and guts" 170–1; "Shakespeare is too *big* for film" 174–5; "size is more than big and loud" 159–61; "speak a soliloquy as if your life depended on it" 169–70; "there is never a Fourth Wall" 158–9; "there is no subtext in Shakespeare" 153–8
"don't report, make a discovery!" 167–8
"don't think about it" exercise 69–71
Double Falsehood 57
"dueling Shakespeare" exercise 102–7
"Duh, Hell-oh, F—k!" exercise 87–9

Earl of Leicester's Men 156
Edward III (or *King Edward III*) 57
"egg on your face" phrase 20
elisions 129
Elizabethan theatre: actors 21–3; audience 16, 19–21; cue acting and scripting 24–5; flags (black, white, red) atop theater 18; leaflets 18; lighting, universal and by candle 18–19; number of productions 24; scrolls (cue scripts) and example from *A Midsummer Night's Dream* 25–31; the stage 16, 18; stage entries for actors 19; stage furniture 18; The Swan Theatre (circa. 1596) 17, 18; thrust stage acting 16, 31–2, 158, 159; women's roles 15–16, 23–4
Elizabeth I, Queen of England 14, 15, 19, 20, 39
"emotion" lesson 89–90; dueling Shakespeare 102–7; grow from the ground up 100; the last line six times 98–100; in-motion, not e-motion 90–4; my cat is dead 94–8, 177; roll on the floor 101–2
English Sumptuary Law, 1574 (The Statutes of Revels) 156–7
epilogues, and use of rhyme verse 131
eros 7
"every line is a new discovery" exercise 75–6
exposition, "don't report, make a discovery!" 167–8

feminine (or weak) endings 127–8, 130
film work: film acting vs. acting Shakespeare 160; Kenneth Branagh's Shakespeare films 147, 175; "less is more" dictum vs. acting Shakespeare 174; and mumbling 65; "Shakespeare is too *big* for film" 174–5
First Folio 15, 25–6, 124, 142

INDEX

flags (atop theater in Elizabethan time) 18
Fletcher, John 45, 55–6, 57
Folger Shakespeare Library 124, 180
Fourth Wall: "there is never a Fourth Wall" 158–9; vs. thrust stage acting 31
F-word 87–8, 150

Globe Theatre (London) 14, 16, 18, 21, 22, 125, 159
glossary of common Shakespearean terminology 180–3
"gobbledygook" exercise 87
Greeks, words for love 7
Greek tragedy 89
groundlings 16
"grow from the ground up" exercise 100
guile, vs. subtext 154–5

Hamlet: Claudius's "A very ribbon in the cap of youth" quote 178; Claudius's prayer 129–31, 187–8; couplets 132–3; Hamlet's "But I have that within which passeth show" scene 132; Hamlet's "mirror up to nature" quote 60, 62; Hamlet's "O, vengeance" quote 69; Hamlet's "rogue and peasant slave" speech 73, 127; Hamlet's "Speak the speech" speech 1–2; Hamlet's "To be, or not to be" speech 8–10, 128, 165, 169; Hamlet's "With all my love I do commend me to you" speech 132–3; play-within-play 131; practice speech (men) 187–8; prose for speeches spoken out of madness 146; soldiers' "Give you good night" scene 125–6; and speaking directly to the audience 32; synopsis 48
hands, "leave your hands *alone*" 168–9
"hang your verse" exercise 83–5
Hellman, Lillian 155
Hemminge, John 15
Henry IV, Part 1: mixture of iambic pentameter and prose 146; practice speech (women) 196–7; synopsis 44
Henry IV, Part 2, synopsis 45
Henry V: Chorus's "O for a Muse of fire" speech 81–2; Chorus's "on your imaginary forces work" line 172; Hostess's "he's not in hell" speech 146–7; Kenneth Branagh's film 175; synopsis 45; use of poetry and prose 118, 131, 145–6; "Wooden O" 16
Henry VI, Part 1: practice speech (women) 195–6; synopsis 42
Henry VI, Part 2: possibly Shakespeare's first play 14; synopsis 41

Henry VI, Part 3, synopsis 42
Henry VIII, synopsis 45–6
Herbert, Mary, Countess of Pembroke (née Sidney) *see* Pembroke, Mary Sidney Herbert, Countess of
hexameters 129
histories (synopses): *Henry IV, Part 1* 44; *Henry IV, Part 2* 45; *Henry V* 45; *Henry VI, Part 1* 42; *Henry VI, Part 2* 41; *Henry VI, Part 3* 42; *Henry VIII* 45–6; *King John* 44; *Richard II* 43; *Richard III* 43
history plays, red flag atop theater 18
Holinshed, Raphael, *Chronicles of England, Scotland and Ireland* 57
Homer, *Iliad* 129
"hop, kneel, crawl, and hug!" exercise 72–3
"howl" exercise 66–8
Hughes, Margaret 23

iambic pentameters: about, terminology, and "doing" it 120–3; alexandrines 129; amphibrachs 121; anapests 121, 128; caesuras 120, 129; dactyls 121, 129; elisions 129; feminine (or weak) endings 127–8, 130; hexameters 129; imperfect lines 126–7; pyrrhics 129; scansion 121, 123, 129–31; shared lines 124–7; sonnets 141; for specific effect and weighty need 146; spondees 127, 129, 130; tetrameters 129; trochees 121, 128
Ibsen, Henrik 155
imperfect lines 126–7
"in-motion, not e-motion" exercise 90–4
intellectual property 25
in-the-round black box 159

James I, King of England 14, 19
Julius Caesar: Plutarch as source 47, 56; senate setting 18; synopsis 47–8

Kempe, Will 22, 38, 61; drawing of on *Nine Daie's Wonder* cover 22
kicking, followed by speaking 73–4
King Edward III (or *Edward III*) 57
King John, synopsis 44
King Lear: description of wind in text 18; Edmund the Bastard silenced from speaking directly to audience 157; "Howl, howl, howl, howl!" scene 66–7; synopsis 49–50
King's Men (formerly Lord Chamberlain's Men) 14, 19, 24; *see also* Lord Chamberlain's Men (later King's Men)

Laban system 86
LaBute, Neil 58
"the last line six times" exercise 98–100
"leave your hands *alone*" 168–9
lessons: aim and advice 62–3, 107–8; warm-up 63–6; *see also* "doing" lesson; "emotion" lesson; "sound" lesson; "verse" lesson
librettos, and intellectual property/copyright 25
lighting, and Elizabethan stage 18–19
Lord Chamberlain's Men (later King's Men) 14, 19, 21, 24, 123, 156; *see also* King's Men (formerly Lord Chamberlain's Men)
love: Greeks' six words for 7; outrageous situations caused by 4–5, 7–8, 89, 176
Love's Labour's Lost: plot totally created by Shakespeare 57; synopsis 36
ludus 7
Luhrmann, Baz, *Romeo + Juliet* 175

Macbeth: "I heard the owl scream" scene 124–5; "Let us seek out some desolate shade" scene and "doing" 161–3; Malcolm's "We shall not spend a large expense of time" passage 117; prose for speeches spoken out of madness 146; Seyton's "The queen, my lord, is dead" scene 167; spell cast by Weird Sisters 128; synopsis 50–1
McKellen, Ian, *Richard III* film 175
made-up words: New Millennium's 150–1; Shakespeare's 147–50; *see also* Shakespearean terminology glossary
"magic if" 3, 5
Manners, Roger, 5th Earl of Rutland 15
Marlowe, Christopher 15
Master of Revels 22
Measure for Measure: capping couplet 133; Claudio's "Ay but to die/'tis too horrible!" speech 172, 177; Duke Vincentio's "Shame to him" speech 132; Isabella's "To whom should I complain?" speech 75, 197–8; practice speech (women) 197–8; "problem play" 34, 41; rhymed verse 132; synopsis 40–1
Meisner, Sanford, Meisner Technique 31
The Merchant of Venice: Al Pacino's film 175; capping couplet 133; plot twists and boy players 23; "problem play" 34; synopsis 37
The Merry Wives of Windsor: Ford's "Epicurean rascal"

speech 87, 173, 189–90; practice speeches (men) 189–91; synopsis 39; use of poetry and prose 118–19

The Method 3, 122, 155

A Midsummer Night's Dream: antithesis and "Pyramus and Thisbe" play-within-play 164; Bottom's "I have had a most rare vision" line 176; cue script examples 26–30; "dueling" scenes 107; Helena's "How happy" speech 80–1, 202–3; Hermia's, Lysander's and Helena's "My good Lysander" scene 134–6; Oberon's "I know a bank" speech 94, 170–1; Ovid as source 56–7; play-within-play 131, 164; practice speech (men) 188–9; practice speeches (women) 202–4; prose for low comedy scene 146; Quince's "here are your parts" quote 60, 97; Quince's "If that may be" quote 21; Quince's "we will have such a prologue" passage 109; rhymed verse 131; synopsis 36–7; "them lines *come* real easy to you" anecdote 12, 178; Titania's changeling child monologue 94

Miller, Arthur, *Death of a Salesman* 33, 44

More, Thomas *see Sir Thomas More*

motivation question 61, 69–70, 97; *see also* subtext

Much Ado About Nothing: Beatrice's and Benedick's "I wonder that you will still be talking" scene 105–6; Benedick's "The world must be peopled!" speech 94, 193; Kenneth Branagh's film 175; practice speeches (men) 192–3; synopsis 37–8

mumbling: and desire to be "real" 160; and "doing film" 65; and The Method 122; and "A Pig in Slop" exercise 174; Stanley Kowalski and mumbling realism (*A Streetcar Named Desire*) 120

musical scores, and intellectual property/copyright 25

Music Theatre International 25

"my cat is dead" exercise 94–8, 177

naturalism 155

New Variorum Shakespeare 180

Nine Daie's Wonder, cover with Will Kempe drawing 22

No Fear Shakespeare 58

Olivier, Laurence 45

O'Neill, Eugene 1

onomatopoeia 86, 93

Othello: couplets 141; Desdemona first time played

by a woman 23; Iago
silenced from speaking
directly to audience 157;
Paul Robeson as 168;
synopsis 49; use of poetry
and prose 118
"outrageous" situations: caused
by love 4–5, 7–8, 89, 176;
defining "outrageous" 5–6;
and doing Shakespeare 8–10;
examples of "outrageous"
plays 33; Shakespeare's
"outrageous" plays 33
Ovid, *Metamorphosis* 56–7

Pacino, Al, *The Merchant of
Venice* film 175
"*paint* the picture" 171–3; "A
Pig in Slop" exercise 173–4
Parks, Suzan-Lori 58
The Passionate Pilgrim 142
pausing 119–20, 168; *see also*
caesuras
The Pelican Shakespeare 124
Pembroke, Mary Sidney
Herbert, Countess of 15
Pembroke, William Herbert,
3rd Earl of Pembroke 142
penny stinkers 16
pentameters *see* iambic
pentameters; trochaic
pentameters
performing, vs. reading 12, 26
Pericles, synopsis 52–3
peripeteia 142
philautia (self-love) 7
philia 7

picking up one's cues 120; and
shared lines 125
"A Pig in Slop" exercise 173–4
the pit 16
platt (call board) 22–3
Playing Shakespeare (John
Barton) 88
plays-within-plays 131, 164
"play the antithesis" exercise
165–7
"play the play," vs.
"Shakespearean" acting 57–8
"play what the scene is *doing*"
161–4
plot twists, and female-playing
actors 23
Plutarch, *Lives* 47, 56
poetic meter 31
poetry *see* blank verse (verse
without rhyme); couplets;
iambic pentameters;
Shakespeare's poetry;
sonnets; "verse" lesson
practice speeches (men):
Hamlet 187–8; *The Merry Wives
of Windsor* 189–91; *A
Midsummer Night's Dream*
188–9; *Much Ado About
Nothing* 192–3; *Romeo and
Juliet* 184–7; *The Two
Gentlemen of Verona* 191–2
practice speeches (women):
All's Well That Ends Well 198;
As You Like It 204–6; *The
Comedy of Errors* 200–1; *Henry
IV, Part 1* 196–7; *Henry VI,
Part 1* 195–6; *Measure for*

Measure 197–8; *A Midsummer Night's Dream* 202–4; *Romeo and Juliet* 194–5; *The Taming of the Shrew* 201–2; *The Tempest* 201; *The Winter's Tale* 199
pragma 7
pretty speeches, "pretty speeches are about blood and guts" 170–1
printing press 25
"problem plays" 33–4, 40, 41, 49, 54
projection 66
prologues, and use of rhyme verse 131
prompter (or theater manager) 22
proscenium stage 31, 158, 159
prose: mixture of poetry and prose 117–19; significance of its use 145–7; "write it in prose" exercise 80–1
public beheadings 20, 156
punctuation, and pausing 120
pyrrhics 129

quatrains 141–2

Rabe, David, *Streamers* 20
Raleigh, Walter 15
The Rape of Lucrece 14, 142; "For more it is than I can well express" passage 176; "'O Peace!' quoth Lucrece" passage 89
realism: carnage in Shakespeare's plays 20; mumbling and desire to be "real" 160; mumbling realism and Stanley Kowalski (*A Streetcar Named Desire*) 120; non-realistic performance style and Shakespeare's plays 24; realistic possibilities in Shakespeare 62
reporting, "don't report, make a discovery!" 167–8
"research" process 58
Richard II: "How long a time lies in one little word!" quote 109; rhymed verse 131; synopsis 43
Richard III: Ian McKellen's film 175; Richard silenced from speaking directly to audience 157; synopsis 43
Robeson, Paul 168
Rogers and Hammerstein Organization 25
role, origin of term 25
"roll on the floor" exercise 101–2
romances (synopses): *Cymbeline* 54–5; *Pericles* 52–3; *The Tempest* 55; *The Two Noble Kinsmen* 55–6; *The Winter's Tale* 53–4
Romeo + Juliet (Baz Luhrmann's film) 175
Romeo and Juliet: balcony scene 137–8; Chorus's "two-hours' traffic of our stage" line 99, 107; Chorus's "Two households" speech 85–6,

184–5; Friar Laurence's and Romeo's "What early tongue so sweet saluteth me?" scene 138–40; Friar Laurence's "I will be brief" speech 167; "Gregory, o' my word, we'll not carry coals" scene 103–5; inspired by Arthur Brooke's poem 57; Juliet's "Come, vial" line 69; Juliet's "My dismal scene' lines 126–7; *ludus* and *eros* in 7; Mercutio's Queen Mab speech 76–9, 173, 185–6; Peter character and laughs 61; practice speeches (men) 184–7; practice speeches (women) 194–5; rhymed verse 131–2; Romeo's and Juliet's first conversation in sonnet form 142–4; synopsis 47
Rose Theatre (London) 14

scansion 121, 123, 129–31
scrolls 25–6, 30–1; *A Midsummer Night's Dream* examples 26–30
self-love (*philautia*) 7
Shakespeare, William: authorship issue 14–15; brief biography 13–15; emotional speeches 90; and outrageous situations caused by love 4–5, 8–10, 33; "problem plays" 33–4, 40, 41, 49, 54; *Sonnets* and sexuality issue 142; source material 56–7; synopses of comedies 34–41; synopses of histories 46–52; synopses of romances 52–7; synopses of tragedies 46–52; works outside canon 57; *see also* doing Shakespeare; Elizabethan theatre; Shakespearean characters; Shakespearean terminology glossary; Shakespeare's poetry
"Shakespearean" acting, vs. "play the play" 57–8
Shakespearean characters, "all Shakespearean characters are *philosophers* and *poets*" 176–7
Shakespearean terminology glossary 180–3
The Shakespeare Book of Lists 148–50
Shakespeare's poetry: "doing" vs. "studying" it 109–10; made-up words 147–51; mixture of poetry and prose 117–19; poetry and "A Pig in Slop" exercise 174; poetry without rhyme, pausing and punctuation 119–20; prose 145–7; rhymed verse and couplets 131–41; sonnets 141–5; *thou* and *you* 110–17; summary 151–2; *see also* blank verse (verse without rhyme); couplets; iambic pentameters; Shakespearean terminology glossary; sonnets
shared lines, and iambic pentameters 124–7

Shaw, George Bernard 1
"sides" 25
Simon, Neil, *The Odd Couple* 33
"sing" exercise 68–9
Sir Thomas More 57
"size is more than big and loud" 159–61
soliloquies, "speak a soliloquy as if your life depended on it" 169–70
songs 131
sonnets: definition and terminology 141–2; "Mark how one string" quote (8.9-10) 86; in *Romeo and Juliet* 142–4; "Shall I compare thee to a summer's day . . . ?" (Sonnet 18) 144; *Sonnets* (1592-1598) 142; "write a sonnet" exercise 144–5
Sophocles 6; *Oedipus Rex* 33
"sound" lesson: "Duh, Hell-oh, F—k!" 87–9; gobbledygook 87; onomatopoeia 86, 93
Southampton, Henry Wriothesley, 3rd Earl of Southampton 142
South Pacific 33
SparkNotes 58
speeches *see* practice speeches (men); practice speeches (women); pretty speeches; soliloquies
spondees 127, 129, 130
stage: in Elizabethan time 16–19; proscenium stage 31, 158, 159; in-the-round black box 159; thrust stage 16, 31–2, 158, 159
Stanislavsky, Konstantin 3, 79, 107, 155
The Statutes of Revels (English Sumptuary Law, 1574) 156–7
storytelling, "*paint* the picture" and "A Pig in Slop" exercise 171–4
Strasberg, Lee 155
Stratford-on-Avon, England 13, 14
Strindberg, August 155
subtext, "there is no subtext in Shakespeare" 153–8
"suspension of disbelief" 32, 159
The Swan Theatre, drawing (circa. 1596) 17, 18

The Taming of the Shrew: "dueling" scenes 107; Katherina's "Unknit that threatening unkind brow" speech 97–8; practice speech (women) 201–2; "study what you most affect" quote 1; synopsis 35
Tams-Witmark 25
"tear the words!" exercise 81–2
The Tempest: Caliban's "I must eat my dinner" speech 72; description of Prospero's foes 18; plot totally created by Shakespeare 57; practice

speech (women) 201; Prospero's "Our revels now are ended" speech 178; songs 131; synopsis 55
tetrameters 129
theater, vs. theatre 11
theater manager (or prompter) 22
Theobald, Lewis 57
thou and *you* 110–17
thrust stage 16, 31–2, 158, 159
Timon of Athens: Plutarch as source 56; "problem play" 34, 49; synopsis 49
Titus Andronicus: depictions of carnage 20; Marcus's "Who is this?" speech 90–4, 96, 99; and outrageous situations caused by love 5; Ovid as source 56–7; and speaking directly to the audience 32; synopsis 46–7; Titus's "doth not the earth o'erflow" passage 4
tragedies, black flag atop theater 18
tragedies (synopses): *Antony and Cleopatra* 51; *Coriolanus* 51–2; *Hamlet* 48; *Julius Caesar* 47–8; *King Lear* 49–50; *Macbeth* 50–1; *Othello* 49; *Romeo and Juliet* 47; *Timon of Athens* 49; *Titus Andronicus* 46–7
Tree, Herbert Beerbohm 5
trochaic pentameters 123
trochees 121, 128

Troilus and Cressida: "problem play" 34; synopsis 39–40; "Things won are done" quote 66
Twelfth Night: capping couplet 133; description of sea storm 18; Malvolio's "Be not afraid of greatness" quote 13; Malvolio's "Daylight and champian" speech 74; Malvolio's "Do you come near me now!" speech 94; Malvolio's "O, ho!" line 68; Olivia's "divers schedules of my beauty" passage 153; plot twists and boy players 23; rhymed verse 131; songs 131; synopsis 38
The Two Gentlemen of Verona: Boccaccio's *The Decameron* as source 57; "kind Julia / unkind Julia" speech 81; Launce's "Crab, my dog" speech 173, 191–2; plot twists and boy players 23; practice speech (men) 191–2; synopsis 35–6
The Two Noble Kinsmen, synopsis 55–6

universal lighting 18–19

Venus and Adonis 14, 142
"verb to verb" exercise 85–6
"verse" lesson 79; hang your verse 83–5; tear the words!

81–2; verb to verb 85–6; write it in prose 80–1
verse without rhyme (blank verse) 90, 118, 119–20, 145, 147; *see also* iambic pentameters; "verse" lesson
viewpoints system 86
violence, "realistic" depictions of 20
"voice" actors 178

warm-up 63–6
weak (or feminine) endings 127–8, 130
whispering 67
white make-up, and lead poisoning 24
Williams, Tennessee, Stanley Kowalski and mumbling realism (*A Streetcar Named Desire*) 120
"willing suspension of disbelief" 32, 159

Wilson, Lanford 155
The Winter's Tale: Bohemian desert setting 18; Camillo's "Here comes Bohemia!" speech 99–100; practice speech (women) 199; "problem play" 34, 54; synopsis 53–4
Witt, Johannes de 17
women's roles: played by boys/men 15–16, 23–4; playing Mercutio 77; *see also* practice speeches (women)
"Wooden O" 16
"wrestle, kick, speak!" exercise 73–4
"write it in prose" exercise 80–1

you and *thou* 110–17
"you are being chased" exercise 74–5